Taste of Home

Brunch

FAVORITES

201 DELICIOUS IDEAS TO START YOUR DAY

D0060654

TASTE OF HOME BOOKS • RDA ENTHUSIAST BRANDS, LLC • MILWAUKEE, WI

Taste of Home Reader's digest

A TASTE OF HOME/READER'S DIGEST BOOK

EDITORIAL

Editor-in-Chief: Catherine Cassidy
Creative Director: Howard Greenberg
Editorial Operations Director: Kerri Balliet

Managing Editor, Print & Digital Books:
Mark Hagen
Associate Creative Director: Edwin Robles Jr.

Editor: Janet Briggs
Art Director: Raeann Sundholm
Layout Designer: Catherine Fletcher
Editorial Production Manager: Dena Ahlers
Copy Chief: Deb Warlaumont Mulvey
Copy Editor: Dulcie Shoener
Contributing Copy Editor: Valerie Phillips
Content Operations Manager: Colleen King
Content Operations Assistant: Shannon Stroud
Executive Assistant: Marie Brannon

Chief Food Editor: Karen Berner
Food Editors: James Schend; Peggy Woodward, RD
Recipe Editors: Mary King; Annie Rundle;
Jenni Sharp, RD; Irene Yeh

Test Kitchen & Food Styling Manager:
Sarah Thompson
Test Cooks: Nicholas Iverson (lead),
Matthew Hass, Lauren Knoelke
Food Stylists: Kathryn Conrad (senior),
Leah Rekau, Shannon Roum
Prep Cooks: Megumi Garcia, Melissa Hansen,
Bethany Van Jacobson, Sara Wirtz

Photography Director: Stephanie Marchese
Photographers: Dan Roberts, Jim Wieland
Photographer/Set Stylist: Grace Natoli Sheldon
Set Stylists: Stacey Genaw, Melissa Haberman,
Dee Dee Jacq

Editorial Business Manager: Kristy Martin
Editorial Business Associate: Samantha Lea Stoeger

BUSINESS
Vice President, Chief Sales Officer:
Mark S. Josephson

General Manager, Taste of Home Cooking School:
Erin Puariea

Vice President, Digital Experience & E-Commerce:
Jennifer Smith

THE READER'S DIGEST ASSOCIATION, INC.
President and Chief Executive Officer:
Bonnie Kintzer
Chief Financial Officer: Colette Chestnut
**Vice President, Chief Operating Officer,
North America:** Howard Halligan
Vice President, Enthusiast Brands, Books & Retail:
Harold Clarke
Vice President, North American Operations:
Philippe Cloutier
Chief Marketing Officer: Leslie Dukker Doty
Vice President, North American Human Resources:
Phyllis E. Gebhardt, SPHR
Vice President, Brand Marketing: Beth Gorry
Vice President, Global Communications: Susan Russ
Vice President, North American Technology:
Aneel Tejwaney
Vice President, Consumer Marketing Planning:
Jim Woods

For other Taste of Home books and products,
visit us at tasteofhome.com.

For more Reader's Digest products and information,
visit rd.com (in the United States)
or see rd.ca (in Canada).

International Standard Book Number:
978-1-61765-365-0
Library of Congress Control Number:
2014948117

Cover Photographer: Grace Natoli Sheldon
Set Stylist: Stacey Genaw
Food Stylist: Leah Rekau

Pictured on front cover:
Apple-Cheddar Pancakes with Bacon, page 94
Pictured on back cover:
Raspberry Almond Coffee Cake, page 159 and
Italian Brunch Torte, page 35
Illustrations on inside cover:
Ohn Mar/Shutterstock.com

Printed in China.
1 3 5 7 9 10 8 6 4 2

LIKE US
facebook.com/tasteofhome

TWEET US
@tasteofhome

FOLLOW US
pinterest.com/taste_of_home

SHOP WITH US
shoptasteofhome.com

SHARE A RECIPE
tasteofhome.com/submit

Blueberry Sour Cream Coffee Cake, page 162
Prosciutto & Cheddar Breakfast Biscuits, page 68

TABLE OF CONTENTS

Maple-Glazed
Sausages,
page 117

Polynesian
Parfaits,
page 200

LET'S DO BRUNCH

Synonymous with deliciously fun get-togethers, brunches are more popular than ever! After all, the eye-opening gatherings offer classic breakfast favorites combined with savory lunch staples, change-of-pace beverages and sweet sensations that keep everyone happy.

Now it's easier than ever to create a memorable morning lineup with *Taste of Home Brunch Favorites*! Here you'll find the perfect items for a friendly brunch buffet, a special

sit-down breakfast or even a quaint coffee with friends. Brunch is about enjoying the moment, so grab a mimosa—and let's celebrate the day!

Try this
**Mascarpone-
Stuffed French
Toast with Triple
Berry Topping**
on page 107.

Welcome your guests to brunch with an assortment of items such as a savory egg bake, muffins, bacon, fruits and a refreshing beverage.

A Pinch of Planning

Most brunches are held from 10 a.m. to 2 p.m., so there isn't much time to prepare before guests arrive. That said, look for recipes that can be made ahead of time. Consider egg bakes, French toast and dishes that set up overnight. Muffins, crescents and scones can be baked the day before and easily warmed in the oven as guests arrive. Deli platters and fruit trays can be assembled and stored in the fridge in advance as well.

Set the table or buffet the night before. Brunch is an ideal time to use your favorite serving pieces, so get them out and determine which pieces will feature which foods. Write notes on pieces of paper and use them to mark platters and bowls so you won't forget in the morning.

Set up a beverage service or bar in a separate location.

For many, beverages are key to brunch. If possible, set up a beverage service or bar in a separate location. This way your guests won't have to balance their plates while pouring a beverage. In addition to juice and coffee, consider serving water, hot and iced tea, Bloody Marys and, of course, champagne!

Brunch Basics

When hosting brunch, it's easy to delight guests. Most will assume you'll serve at least one entree, a side dish or two, fruit, a bread, and coffee and juice. Eggs are well-suited for morning get-togethers because they cook in minutes and can be used in a variety of dishes. Here are a few pointers to help create fabulous egg dishes.

Serve an easy egg bake with some extras, like this **Eggs Benedict Casserole** on page 41, or an all-in-one dish such as **Southwest Hash with Adobo-Lime Crema** on page 60.

Scrambled Eggs

Pour beaten egg mixture into the prepared skillet. As the eggs start to set, gently pull them across the pan with an inverted spatula or wooden spoon, forming large soft curds. Continue lifting and folding the eggs until the mixture has thickened and no visible liquid remains.

Poached Eggs

Place 2-3 inches of water in a skillet with high sides; add 1 tablespoon vinegar. (Acidic poaching liquid makes it easier to get good results.) Bring to a boil; reduce heat and simmer gently. Break a cold egg into a cup or saucer; holding the cup close to the surface of the water, slip egg into water. Repeat with next egg.

Omelets

Heat oil or butter in a 10-inch nonstick skillet over medium-high heat until hot. Tilt pan to ensure entire bottom is coated with butter. Add egg mixture to skillet (mixture should set immediately at the edges). As eggs start to set, push the cooked edges toward the center, letting the uncooked portion flow underneath. Repeat until eggs are set and there's no visible liquid.

Spoon filling on top of one half; fold the other half over the filling and cook to desired doneness. Slide the omelet onto a plate.

Over-Easy Eggs

Break egg into a cup and gently slide into pan. Reduce heat to low. Cook slowly, uncovered, until the whites are completely firm and yolks begin to thicken but are not hard. Carefully slide a spatula under the egg and flip. Continue cooking, uncovered, until desired doneness is reached.

Doneness of Baked Eggs

Test egg dishes containing beaten eggs—like quiche, strata or custard—for doneness by inserting a knife near the center of the dish. If the knife comes out clean, the eggs are cooked.

BACON FOR A CROWD

Slices of crispy bacon are a favorite accompaniment to eggs, pancakes and waffles. Cooked bacon loses its crisp texture when refrigerated, however, so it's not an ideal make-ahead food. Frying up a lot of bacon as guests arrive isn't ideal either, so consider this simple solution.

Preheat the oven to 400°. Line one or two baking sheets with foil, and arrange bacon slices in a single layer on the sheets. Bake 15-20 minutes or until crisp. Switch position of baking sheets halfway through cooking. Remove the sheets from the oven carefully.

Eye-Opening Ideas

Brunches can be formal or casual, elegant or simple. They're suitable for an array of celebrations and themes, and they make a perfect fit for busy schedules. See the opposite page for a few menu suggestions.

Enjoy a delicious sweet, such as **Raspberry Almond Coffee Cake** on page 159, when the girls come over for coffee, or spice up mornings with **Green Chili Breakfast Burritos** on page 44.

Easy Cappuccino, page 29
Turkey Swiss Quiche, page 65

MENU SUGGESTIONS

Friendly Sunday Soiree
- ☐ Bacon Cinnamon Buns, 144
- ☐ Banana Fruit Compote, 201
- ☐ Amish Breakfast Casserole, 39
- ☐ Blueberry Cheesecake Flapjacks, 111
- ☐ Savory Apple-Chicken Sausage, 130
- ☐ Coffee Milk, Regular Milk, Coffee, Tea & Orange Juice

Coffee Klatch
- ☐ Vanilla Fruit Salad, 200
- ☐ Almond Coffee Cake, 143
- ☐ Classic Fruit Kolaches, 172
- ☐ White Chocolate Macadamia Muffins, 151
- ☐ Turkey Swiss Quiche, 65
- ☐ Easy Cappuccino, 29; Frappe Mocha, 18; Chai Tea, 33

Baby Shower
- ☐ Cucumber Punch, 14
- ☐ Berry & Yogurt Phyllo Nests, 201
- ☐ Brie and Prosciutto Tart, 46
- ☐ Breakfast Skewers, 129
- ☐ Blueberry Sour Cream Coffee Cake, 162
- ☐ Coffee, Tea & Assorted Juices

Spring Celebration
- ☐ Citrus Mint Cooler, 18
- ☐ Coconut Tropical Fruit Salad, 188
- ☐ Raspberry Streusel Coffee Cake, 164
- ☐ Spiral Omelet Supreme, 56
- ☐ Baked Canadian-Style Ham, 121
- ☐ Coffee, Tea & Milk

Winter Warm-Up
- ☐ Dill Bloody Marys, 25
- ☐ Latkes with Lox, 105
- ☐ Sausage Sandwich Squares, 177
- ☐ Spinach Hash Brown Frittata, 54
- ☐ Buttermilk Angel Biscuits, 179
- ☐ Easy Espresso, 11 & Sunburst Spiced Tea, 19

Girls Gab Fest
- ☐ Champagne Fruit Punch, 23
- ☐ Strawberry Mascarpone Crepes, 88
- ☐ Maple-Glazed Sausages, 117
- ☐ Pecan Apple Strudel, 167
- ☐ Coffee & Tea

Slumber Party Wake-Up
- ☐ Morning Fruit Salad, 191
- ☐ Banana Chip Pancakes, 108
- ☐ Hot Malted Chocolate, 28 & Apple Juice

9

Creamy
Caramel Mocha

Morning
Joe & More

CREAMY CARAMEL MOCHA

Indulge in a sweet sensation at brunch...or any time at all! With whipped cream and a butterscotch drizzle, this mocha treat will impress guests whether you serve it morning, noon or night.

—*TASTE OF HOME* TEST KITCHEN

START TO FINISH: 20 MIN.
MAKES: 6 SERVINGS

- ½ **cup heavy whipping cream**
- 1 **tablespoon confectioners' sugar**
- 1 **teaspoon vanilla extract, divided**
- ¼ **cup Dutch-processed cocoa**
- 1½ **cups half-and-half cream**
- 4 **cups hot strong brewed coffee**
- ½ **cup caramel flavoring syrup**
  Butterscotch-caramel ice cream topping

1. In a small bowl, beat whipping cream until it begins to thicken. Add confectioners' sugar and ½ teaspoon vanilla; beat until stiff peaks form.

2. In a large saucepan over medium heat, whisk cocoa and half-and-half cream until smooth. Heat until bubbles form around sides of the pan. Whisk in coffee, caramel syrup and the remaining vanilla. Top each serving with whipped cream; drizzle with the butterscotch topping.

NOTE *This recipe was tested with Torani brand flavoring syrup. Look for it in the coffee section.*

EASY ESPRESSO

Capture the classic taste of espresso without the hassle of expensive brewing equipment! For best flavor, serve espresso immediately. Pour any leftover espresso into ice cube trays and freeze to use later in cold drinks.

—*TASTE OF HOME* TEST KITCHEN

START TO FINISH: 10 MIN.
MAKES: 4 SERVINGS

- ½ **cup ground coffee (French or other dark roast)**
- 1½ **cups cold water**
  Lemon twists, optional

Place ground coffee in the filter of a drip coffeemaker. Add water; brew according to manufacturer's instructions. Serve immediately in espresso cups. If desired, serve with lemon twists.

NOTE *This recipe was tested with Starbucks French Roast ground coffee.*

MEXICAN HOT CHOCOLATE

This delicious, not-too-sweet hot chocolate is richly flavored with cocoa and delicately seasoned with spices. The cinnamon and chocolate flavors blend wonderfully!

—KATHY YOUNG WEATHERFORD, TX

START TO FINISH: 10 MIN.
MAKES: 4 SERVINGS

- ¼ **cup baking cocoa**
- 2 **tablespoons brown sugar**
- 1 **cup boiling water**
- ¼ **teaspoon ground cinnamon**
  Dash ground cloves or nutmeg
- 3 **cups milk**
- 1 **teaspoon vanilla extract**
  Whipped cream
  Whole cinnamon sticks

1. In a small saucepan, mix cocoa and sugar; stir in water. Bring to a boil. Reduce heat; cook 2 minutes, stirring constantly.
2. Add the cinnamon and cloves; stir in milk. Simmer 5 minutes (do not boil). Whisk in vanilla. Pour hot chocolate into mugs; top with whipped cream. Use cinnamon sticks for stirrers.

FESTIVE MIMOSA

Add a splash of color to your brunch table with this rosy Mimosa. It has a fantastic sweet-tart taste.

—JESSIE SARRAZIN LIVINGSTON, MT

START TO FINISH: 5 MIN.
MAKES: 1 SERVING

- 1 **tablespoon red coarse sugar**
- ½ **ounce raspberry liqueur**
- 2 **ounces ruby red grapefruit juice**
- 2 **ounces champagne**
  Grapefruit twist

1. Sprinkle sugar on a plate. Moisten the rim of a champagne flute with water; hold glass upside down and dip the rim into sugar.
2. Pour the raspberry liqueur and grapefruit juice into the glass; top with the champagne. Garnish with a grapefruit twist.

MIMOSA FOR A CROWD

To make a batch of Mimosas (12 servings), slowly pour one bottle (750 milliliters) of chilled champagne into a pitcher. Stir in 3 cups cranberry juice and ¾ cup raspberry liqueur.

Mexican
Hot Chocolate

CUCUMBER PUNCH

PREP: 10 MIN. + CHILLING
MAKES: 25 SERVINGS (4¾ QUARTS)

- **2 medium cucumbers**
- **3 cups water**
- **1 can (12 ounces) frozen lemonade concentrate, thawed**
- **2 liters diet ginger ale, chilled**
- **4½ cups diet grapefruit or citrus soda, chilled**

1. With a zester or fork, score cucumbers lengthwise; cut widthwise into thin slices. In a large pitcher, combine the water and lemonade concentrate; add cucumbers. Cover and refrigerate overnight.

2. Just before serving, transfer cucumber mixture to a punch bowl; stir in ginger ale and grapefruit soda.

I first tried this wonderfully unique beverage at a ladies luncheon, and have since served it many times. Folks usually request copies of the recipe.

—RENEE OLSON KENDRICK, ID

SPICED APPLE TEA

I love to try new recipes for my husband and our friends. This spiced tea is one of our favorites. I like to serve it warm, but it's also nice served chilled over ice.

—SHARON DELANEY-CHRONIS
SOUTH MILWAUKEE, WI

START TO FINISH: 25 MIN.
MAKES: 5 SERVINGS

- 2 **cups unsweetened apple juice**
- 6 **whole cloves**
- 1 **cinnamon stick (3 inches)**
- 3 **cups water**
- 5 **individual tea bags**
  Additional cinnamon sticks (3 inches), optional

1. In a small saucepan, bring the first three ingredients to a boil. Reduce heat; simmer, uncovered, 10-15 minutes.
2. Meanwhile, in a large saucepan, bring water to a boil. Remove from heat; add tea bags. Cover and steep 5 minutes. Discard tea bags. Strain juice mixture, discarding cloves and cinnamon. Stir into tea. Serve warm, with additional cinnamon sticks if desired.

ICED COFFEE LATTE

This is a refreshing alternative to regular hot coffee and is much more economical than store-bought coffee drinks. Sweetened condensed milk and a hint of chocolate lend a special touch.

—HEATHER NANDELL JOHNSTON, IA

START TO FINISH: 10 MIN.
MAKES: 8 SERVINGS

- ½ **cup instant coffee granules**
- ½ **cup boiling water**
- 4 **cups chocolate milk**
- 2 **cups cold water**
- 1 **can (14 ounces) sweetened condensed milk**
  Ice cubes

In a large bowl, dissolve coffee in boiling water. Stir in chocolate milk, cold water and condensed milk. Serve over ice.

REMOVING TEA & COFFEE STAINS FROM CUPS

Do you have ring around the cup from tea and coffee? It's easy to remove those stains. Sprinkle some baking soda in the cup, add enough water to make a paste, then rub with a cloth until the stain is removed. Rinse, wash and dry, and the cup will sparkle like new.

VANILLA ALMOND HOT COCOA

Treat family and friends to this rich homemade cocoa. It will warm even the coldest winter's chill!

—VICKI HOLLOWAY JOELTON, TN

START TO FINISH: 15 MIN.
MAKES: 10 SERVINGS (2½ QUARTS)

- 1 **cup sugar**
- ⅔ **cup baking cocoa**
- ¼ **teaspoon salt**
- 8 **cups 2% milk**
- ⅔ **cup water**
- 2 **teaspoons vanilla extract**
- ½ **teaspoon almond extract**
  Miniature marshmallows, optional

In a large saucepan, combine the sugar, cocoa and salt. Stir in milk and water. Cook and stir over medium heat until heated through. Remove from heat; stir in extracts. If desired, top each serving with marshmallows.

Vanilla Almond
Hot Cocoa

HOT COCOA TOPPERS

Marshmallows are the go-to topping for hot cocoa. If you'd like to be a little more daring, try one of these ideas: a small scoop of ice cream, strips of orange zest, chocolate shavings, hot sauce or even jalapeno pepper rings.

FRAPPE MOCHA

Coffee ice cubes add body to this refreshing drink. What a treat!

—BEVERLY COYDE GASPORT, NY

PREP: 5 MIN. + FREEZING
MAKES: 2 SERVINGS

- 1 teaspoon instant coffee granules
- ¼ cup boiling water
- 1 cup fat-free milk
- 4½ teaspoons chocolate syrup
- ½ cup crushed ice
  Whipped topping and additional chocolate syrup, optional

1. In a small bowl, dissolve coffee granules in water. Pour into an ice cube tray; freeze.

2. In a blender, combine the milk, chocolate syrup and coffee ice cubes. Cover and process until smooth. Add crushed ice; blend.

3. Pour into chilled glasses; serve immediately. If desired, garnish with whipped topping and additional chocolate syrup.

CITRUS MINT COOLER

My grandmother made this change-of-pace cooler for hot summer days. The family would relax on her Oklahoma porch, enjoying each sip. Here in California, my family has found equal enjoyment, relaxing in the shade with tall glasses of the thirst-quenching delight.

—KATHY BURKHOLDER BAKERSFIELD, CA

PREP: 30 MIN. + CHILLING
MAKES: ABOUT 15 SERVINGS

- 2½ cups water
- 2 cups sugar
- 1 cup lemon juice (about 6 lemons)
- 1 cup orange juice (about 6 oranges)
- 10 mint sprigs
- 1 bottle (32 ounces) ginger ale, chilled
  Cold water
  Ice cubes

1. Place first five ingredients in a large saucepan; bring to a boil, stirring until sugar is dissolved. Cover; remove from heat and let steep until cool. Strain. Cover and refrigerate.

2. To serve, fill chilled glasses or a pitcher with equal amounts of fruit juice, ginger ale and cold water. Add ice and serve immediately.

BRUNCH NOTES

SUNBURST SPICED TEA

Here, oranges and a lemon lend a lovely citrus flavor to ordinary black tea.

—*TASTE OF HOME* TEST KITCHEN

START TO FINISH: 25 MIN.
MAKES: 4 SERVINGS

- 2 **medium oranges**
- 1 **medium lemon**
- 4 **cardamom pods**
- 4 **whole cloves**
- 4 **teaspoons English breakfast tea leaves or other black tea leaves**
- 4 **cups boiling water**

1. Using a citrus zester, remove peel from oranges and lemon in long narrow strips. (Save fruit for another use.) Place peel strips, cardamom and cloves in a large bowl. With the end of a wooden spoon handle, crush mixture until aromas are released.

2. Add tea leaves and boiling water. Cover and steep for 6 minutes. Strain tea, discarding the peel mixture. Serve immediately.

Mango
Smoothies

MANGO SMOOTHIES

Treat yourself to this yummy blend of mango, pineapple, banana and honey. The yogurt makes it rich and creamy, but a serving has only 2 grams of fat!

—TASTE OF HOME TEST KITCHEN

START TO FINISH: 10 MIN. • **MAKES:** 2 SERVINGS

- ½ cup unsweetened pineapple juice
- 2 cups frozen chopped peeled mangoes
- ½ medium ripe banana
- ½ cup reduced-fat plain yogurt
- 1 tablespoon honey

In a blender, combine all the ingredients; cover and process until smooth. Pour into chilled glasses; serve immediately.

COFFEE MILK

After one sip, you'll see why this is the official drink of Rhode Island—it's just delectable!

—TASTE OF HOME TEST KITCHEN

PREP: 10 MIN. • **COOK:** 35 MIN. + CHILLING
MAKES: 4 SERVINGS (1 CUP SYRUP)

- ½ cup finely ground coffee
- 2 cups cold water
- 1 cup sugar

EACH SERVING

- 1 cup cold 2% milk

1. Place ground coffee in filter basket of a drip coffeemaker. Add 2 cups cold water to water reservoir and brew according to manufacturer's directions.

2. In a small saucepan, combine coffee and sugar; bring to a boil. Reduce heat; simmer until reduced by half, about 30 minutes. Remove from heat; transfer to a small bowl or covered container. Refrigerate, covered, until cold or up to 2 weeks.

TO PREPARE COFFEE MILK *In a tall glass, mix 1 cup milk and 2-4 tablespoons coffee milk syrup.*

Champagne
Fruit Punch

CHAMPAGNE FRUIT PUNCH

Toast the happy couple at your next bridal shower with a fun and fruity drink! It's the perfect refreshment.

—KELLY TRAN SALEM, OR

START TO FINISH: 10 MIN.
MAKES: 16 SERVINGS (¾ CUP EACH)

- 2 **cups fresh or frozen raspberries**
- 1 **can (12 ounces) frozen orange juice concentrate, thawed**
- 1 **can (12 ounces) frozen cherry pomegranate juice concentrate, thawed**
- 1 **can (6 ounces) unsweetened pineapple juice, chilled**
- 1 **medium lemon, thinly sliced**
- 1 **bottle (1 liter) club soda, chilled**
- 1 **bottle (750 milliliters) champagne, chilled**

In a punch bowl, combine the first five ingredients. Slowly stir in club soda and champagne. Serve immediately.

CHILD-FRIENDLY FRUIT PUNCH

To serve the Champagne Fruit Punch at a family party, substitute 3 cups chilled sparkling white grape juice for the champagne.

WINTER HERB TEA MIX

START TO FINISH: 10 MIN.
MAKES: 18 SERVINGS
(9 TABLESPOONS TEA MIX)

- 6 **tablespoons dried mint**
- 1 **tablespoon dried sage leaves**
- 1 **tablespoon dried rosemary, crushed**
- 1 **tablespoon dried thyme**

ADDITIONAL INGREDIENTS (FOR EACH SERVING)

- 1 **cup boiling water**
- 1 **teaspoon honey**
- 1 **lemon wedge**

In a small airtight container, combine the herbs. Store in a cool dry place up to 6 months.

TO PREPARE TEA *Place 1½ teaspoons tea mix in a glass measuring cup. With the end of a wooden spoon handle, crush mixture until aromas are released. Add boiling water. Cover and steep 10 minutes. Strain tea into a mug, discarding herbs. Stir in honey; serve with lemon.*

> This caffeine-free option is a blend of mint, sage, rosemary, thyme and honey that melts away any day's troubles.
> —**SUE GRONHOLZ** BEAVER DAM, WI

HOT SPICED GREEN TEA

With ginger, lemon and honey, this tea is ideal for any time of day or occasion.

—TASTE OF HOME TEST KITCHEN

START TO FINISH: 15 MIN.
MAKES: 4 SERVINGS

- 2 **cinnamon sticks (3 inches)**
- 4 **individual green tea bags**
- ½ **teaspoon minced fresh gingerroot**
- ½ **teaspoon grated lemon peel**
- 4 **cardamom pods, crushed**
- 4 **cups boiling water**
- 2 **tablespoons honey**

In a large bowl, combine the first five ingredients. Add boiling water. Cover and steep for 5-6 minutes. Strain, discarding tea bags and spices. Stir honey into tea. Serve immediately.

FRENCH VANILLA MOCHA

My husband and I have spent hours trying to create coffeehouse drinks, and this is the closest we've come. You can use any creamer to change the taste.

—LORI STICKLING BLOOMINGTON, IL

START TO FINISH: 10 MIN.
MAKES: 2 SERVINGS

- 2 **tablespoons instant coffee granules**
- 2 **teaspoons chocolate syrup**
- 1½ **cups 2% milk**
- ½ **cup refrigerated French vanilla coffee creamer**

Divide coffee granules and chocolate syrup between two mugs; set aside. In a microwave-safe bowl, mix milk and coffee creamer. Microwave, uncovered, on high 1-2 minutes or until hot. Ladle into mugs; stir until coffee granules are dissolved. Serve immediately.

DILL BLOODY MARYS

With a nice level of pepper and just enough dill from the pickle, these Bloody Marys are sure to please. Fun garnishes make them like a meal unto themselves!

—JAY FERKOVICH GREEN BAY, WI

START TO FINISH: 10 MIN.
MAKES: 2 SERVINGS

- 1½ **cups Clamato juice, chilled**
- 2 **tablespoons dill pickle juice**
- 1 **tablespoon Worcestershire sauce**
- ¼ **teaspoon celery salt**
- ⅛ **to ¼ teaspoon pepper**
- ⅛ **teaspoon hot pepper sauce**
- ¼ **cup vodka, optional**
  Ice cubes
- 2 **celery ribs**
- 2 **pepperoni-flavored meat snack sticks**
- 2 **dill pickle spears**
- 2 **pitted ripe olives**

In a small pitcher, combine the first six ingredients. If desired, stir in vodka. Pour into two glasses filled with ice; garnish with celery, snack sticks, pickles and olives.

BRUNCH NOTES

_____
_____
_____
_____
_____
_____
_____
_____
_____
_____
_____
_____
_____
_____
_____
_____
_____
_____
_____
_____
_____
_____
_____
_____
_____
_____
_____
_____
_____
_____
_____
_____
_____
_____
_____
_____
_____

BERRY SMOOTHIES

Smooth out the morning rush with a boost of berries. This delightfully balanced beverage is tart, tangy and sweet, so there's no reason to add any extra sugar.

—ELISABETH LARSEN PLEASANT GROVE, UT

START TO FINISH: 5 MIN. • **MAKES:** 5 SERVINGS

- 2 **cups cranberry juice**
- 2 **containers (6 ounces each) raspberry yogurt**
- 1 **cup frozen unsweetened raspberries**
- 1 **cup frozen unsweetened blueberries**
- 8 **ice cubes**

In a blender, combine all ingredients; cover and process 30-45 seconds or until blended. Pour into chilled glasses; serve immediately.

STRAWBERRY LIME SMOOTHIES

Peak-of-freshness strawberries make this drink a summer staple. Garnish each glass with a lime slice.

—ELIZABETH JOHNSON GREENVILLE, SC

START TO FINISH: 5 MIN. • **MAKES:** 3 SERVINGS

- ½ **cup 2% milk**
- 2 **to 4 tablespoons lime juice**
- 2 **cups fresh strawberries, hulled and halved**
- 1 **cup (8 ounces) strawberry yogurt**
- 2 **tablespoons honey**
- ½ **teaspoon ground cinnamon**

In a blender, combine all ingredients; cover and process until smooth. Pour into chilled glasses. Serve immediately.

Berry Smoothies

HOT MALTED CHOCOLATE

There's nothing better on a cold day than a steaming mug of rich hot chocolate. Malted milk powder adds a nice touch to this yummy version.

—CHRISTY MEINECKE MANSFIELD, TX

START TO FINISH: 20 MIN.
MAKES: 5 SERVINGS

- 4 **cups 2% milk**
- 1 **cup heavy whipping cream**
- ½ **cup sugar**
- 1 **cup milk chocolate chips**
- ⅓ **cup malted milk powder**
- 2 **teaspoons vanilla extract**

1. In a large saucepan, heat milk over medium heat until bubbles form around sides of pan.

2. Meanwhile, in a small bowl, beat cream until it begins to thicken. Add sugar; beat until soft peaks form.

3. Whisk chocolate chips and malted milk powder into milk until chocolate is melted. Remove from heat; whisk in vanilla. Pour into mugs. Spoon whipped cream over the top.

A.M. RUSH ESPRESSO SMOOTHIE

Want an early-morning pick-me-up that's good for you, too? Fruit and flaxseed give this sweet espresso a nutritious twist.
—AIMEE WILSON CLOVIS, CA

START TO FINISH: 10 MIN.
MAKES: 1 SERVING

- ½ cup cold fat-free milk
- 1 tablespoon vanilla flavoring syrup
- 1 cup ice cubes
- ½ medium banana, cut up
- 1 to 2 teaspoons instant espresso powder
- 1 teaspoon ground flaxseed
- 1 teaspoon baking cocoa

In a blender, combine all ingredients; cover and process 1-2 minutes or until blended. Pour into a chilled glass; serve immediately.
NOTE *This recipe was tested with Torani brand flavoring syrup. Look for it in the coffee section.*

CHOCOLATE WHIPPED CREAM

For a double shot of chocolate in your favorite hot cocoa, top it with chocolate whipped cream. To make it, beat ½ cup cold heavy whipping cream until it begins to thicken. Add 2 tablespoons chocolate syrup; beat until stiff peaks form.

EASY CAPPUCCINO

A cappuccino is one part espresso mixed with one part steamed milk, then topped with one part foamed milk. This recipe lets you create this popular beverage at home without specialized equipment.
—*TASTE OF HOME* TEST KITCHEN

START TO FINISH: 10 MIN.
MAKES: 1 SERVING

- ½ cup milk
- ⅓ cup hot brewed Easy Espresso (page 11)

1. Place milk in a 1-cup microwave-safe measuring cup. Microwave, uncovered, on high 1 minute or until milk is hot and small bubbles form around edge of cup.
2. Place a metal whisk in cup; whisk vigorously by holding whisk handle loosely between palms and quickly rubbing hands back and forth. Remove foam to a small measuring cup as it forms. Continue whisking until foam measures ⅓ cup; set aside.
3. Pour Easy Espresso into a mug; pour in remaining hot milk. Spoon foam over top and serve immediately.
NOTE *You may also use a portable mixer with whisk attachment to froth the milk. This recipe was tested in a 1,100-watt microwave.*

HAZELNUT COFFEE

A rich blend of flavors—coffee, hazelnut and a bit of chocolate—makes this eye-opener absolutely sensational. It is ideal for breakfast or brunch, but is also wonderful for a quiet moment at the end of the day.

—FRIEDA BLIESNER MCALLEN, TX

START TO FINISH: 15 MIN.
MAKES: 4 SERVINGS

- 4 **cups brewed coffee**
- ¼ **cup hazelnut flavoring syrup**
- 1 **tablespoon sugar**
- ⅛ **teaspoon ground cinnamon**
- ¼ **cup heavy whipping cream**
- 1 **tablespoon Nutella**

1. In a large saucepan, combine the coffee, flavoring syrup, sugar and cinnamon; heat through. Divide coffee mixture among four mugs.
2. In a small bowl, beat cream and Nutella until thickened. Gently spoon onto tops of drinks. Serve immediately.
NOTE *This recipe was tested with Torani brand flavoring syrup. Look for it in the coffee section.*

KEEPING COFFEE FRESH

A good cup of coffee starts with fresh coffee. Once a container is open, coffee does start to lose flavor. Store open containers of ground, instant and freeze-dried coffee in the refrigerator up to 3 weeks. For longer storage, place in the freezer.

Hazelnut
Coffee

Tropical
Lime Smoothies

TROPICAL LIME SMOOTHIES

Bring a touch of the tropics to your morning ritual with this refreshing, tart beverage.
—*TASTE OF HOME* TEST KITCHEN

START TO FINISH: 10 MIN. • **MAKES:** 3 SERVINGS

- 1¼ cups milk
- ¼ cup lime juice
- 1 pint coconut sorbet

In a blender, combine all the ingredients; cover and process until smooth. Pour into chilled glasses; serve immediately.

CHAI TEA

Warm up a chilly evenings—or any day at all—with this inviting tea. The spices really come through, and it's even more delicious when stirred with a cinnamon stick.
—KELLY PACOWTA DANBURY, CT

START TO FINISH: 20 MIN. • **MAKES:** 4 SERVINGS

- 4 whole cloves
- 2 whole peppercorns
- 4 individual tea bags
- 4 teaspoons sugar
- ¼ teaspoon ground ginger
- 1 cinnamon stick (3 inches)
- 2½ cups boiling water
- 2 cups milk

1. Place cloves and peppercorns in a large bowl; with the end of a wooden spoon handle, crush spices until aromas are released.
2. Add the tea bags, sugar, ginger, cinnamon stick and boiling water. Cover and steep for 6 minutes. Meanwhile, in a small saucepan, heat the milk.
3. Strain tea, discarding spices and tea bags. Stir in hot milk. Pour into mugs.

BRUNCH NOTES

Italian
Brunch Torte

Incredible
Eggs

ITALIAN BRUNCH TORTE

We always serve this impressive layered breakfast bake with a salad of mixed greens and tomato wedges. It's one of our most requested dishes, and can be served warm or cold.

—**DANNY DIAMOND** FARMINGTON HILLS, MI

PREP: 50 MIN. • **BAKE:** 1 HOUR + STANDING
MAKES: 12 SERVINGS

- 2 **tubes (8 ounces each) refrigerated crescent rolls, divided**
- 1 **teaspoon olive oil**
- 1 **package (6 ounces) fresh baby spinach**
- 1 **cup sliced fresh mushrooms**
- 7 **eggs**
- 1 **cup grated Parmesan cheese**
- 2 **teaspoons Italian seasoning**
- ⅛ **teaspoon pepper**
- ½ **pound thinly sliced deli ham**
- ½ **pound thinly sliced hard salami**
- ½ **pound sliced provolone cheese**
- 2 **jars (12 ounces each) roasted sweet red peppers, drained, sliced and patted dry**

1. Preheat oven to 350°. Place a greased 9-in. springform pan on a double thickness of heavy-duty foil (about 18 in. square). Securely wrap foil around pan. Unroll one tube of crescent dough and separate into triangles. Press onto bottom of prepared pan to form a crust, sealing seams well. Bake 10-15 minutes or until set.

2. Meanwhile, in a large skillet, heat oil over medium-high heat. Add spinach and mushrooms; cook and stir until mushrooms are tender. Drain on several layers of paper towels, blotting well. In a large bowl, whisk six eggs, Parmesan cheese, Italian seasoning and pepper.

3. Layer crust with half of the ham, salami, provolone cheese, red peppers and spinach mixture. Pour half of the egg mixture over the top. Repeat layers; top with remaining egg mixture.

4. On a work surface, unroll and separate remaining crescent dough into triangles. Press together to form a circle and seal seams; place over filling. Whisk remaining egg; brush over dough.

5. Bake, uncovered, 1 to 1¼ hours or until a thermometer reads 160°, covering loosely with foil if needed to prevent overbrowning. Carefully loosen sides from pan with a knife; remove rim from pan. Let stand 20 minutes.

CHORIZO SALSA OMELET

Just a few ingredients jazz up a basic omelet and make it delish!

—*TASTE OF HOME* TEST KITCHEN

START TO FINISH: 20 MIN.
MAKES: 1 SERVING

- 1 **tablespoon butter**
- 3 **eggs**
- 3 **tablespoons water**
- ⅛ **teaspoon salt**
- ⅛ **teaspoon pepper**
- ¼ **cup cooked chorizo or sausage**
- 2 **tablespoons chunky salsa**

1. In a small nonstick skillet, melt butter over medium-high heat. Whisk the eggs, water, salt and pepper. Add egg mixture to skillet (mixture should set immediately at edges).

2. As eggs set, push cooked edges toward the center, letting uncooked portion flow underneath. When the eggs are set, spoon chorizo and salsa on one side; fold other side over filling. Slide omelet onto a plate.

_____
_____
_____
_____
_____
_____
_____
_____
_____
_____
_____
_____
_____
_____
_____
_____
_____
_____
_____
_____
_____
_____
_____
_____
_____
_____
_____
_____
_____
_____
_____
_____
_____
_____
_____
_____
_____

HUEVOS RANCHEROS WITH TOMATILLO SAUCE

My husband and I visited Cuernavaca, Mexico, a few years ago and had huevos rancheros for breakfast while there. My husband loved it so much that he asked me to cook it for him when we got home. This is my version, which is suited to my family's preference for sunny-side-up eggs, but poached or scrambled eggs would also be good.

—CHERYL WOODSON LIBERTY, MO

START TO FINISH: 25 MIN. • **MAKES:** 8 SERVINGS

- 5 **tomatillos, husks removed, halved**
- 2 **tablespoons coarsely chopped onion**
- 1 **to 2 serrano peppers, halved**
- 3 **garlic cloves, peeled**
- 1 **teaspoon chicken bouillon granules**
- 1 **can (15 ounces) Southwestern black beans, undrained**
- 8 **eggs**
- 4 **ounces manchego cheese, shredded**
- 8 **tostada shells, warmed**
- ½ **cup sour cream**
  Chopped tomato, sliced avocado and minced fresh cilantro, optional

1. Place the tomatillos, onion, pepper, garlic and bouillon in a food processor. Cover and process until mixture is finely chopped; set aside. In a small saucepan, mash beans. Cook on low until heated through, stirring occasionally.

2. Meanwhile, break eggs in batches into a large nonstick skillet coated with cooking spray. Cover and cook over low heat 5-7 minutes or until eggs are set. Sprinkle with cheese.

3. To serve, spread beans over tostada shells; top with eggs, tomatillo sauce and sour cream. Garnish with tomato, avocado and cilantro if desired.

NOTE *Wear disposable gloves when cutting hot peppers; the oils can burn skin. Avoid touching your face.*

Huevos Rancheros
with Tomatillo Sauce

CARAMELIZED MUSHROOM AND ONION FRITTATA

When I was young, my grandmother used to make buttery sauteed mushrooms for me. These days, I enjoy them in a hearty breakfast frittata.
—**MELISSA DANTONIO** POUGHKEEPSIE, NY

PREP: 15 MIN. • **COOK:** 45 MIN.
MAKES: 4 SERVINGS

- 1 **pound sliced fresh mushrooms**
- 1 **medium red onion, chopped**
- 3 **tablespoons butter**
- 3 **tablespoons olive oil**
- 1 **shallot, chopped**
- 1 **garlic clove, minced**
- ½ **cup shredded cheddar cheese**
- ¼ **cup shredded Parmesan cheese**
- 8 **eggs**
- 3 **tablespoons heavy whipping cream**
- ¼ **teaspoon salt**
- ¼ **teaspoon pepper**

1. In a 10-in. ovenproof skillet, saute mushrooms and onion in butter and oil until softened. Reduce heat to medium-low; cook 30 minutes or until deep golden brown, stirring occasionally. Add shallot and garlic; cook 1 minute longer.

2. Reduce heat; sprinkle with cheeses. In a bowl, whisk eggs, cream, salt and pepper; pour over top. Cover and cook 4-6 minutes or until eggs are nearly set.

3. Uncover skillet. Broil 3-4 in. from heat 2-3 minutes or until the eggs are completely set. Let stand 5 minutes. Cut into wedges.

POTATO & BACON FRITTATA

This filling dish is so versatile. You can serve it with pesto or fresh salsa, and it's tasty with almost any type of cheese.
—**MARIELA PETROSKI** HELENA, MT

PREP: 30 MIN. • **BAKE:** 20 MIN. + STANDING
MAKES: 8 SERVINGS

- 10 **eggs**
- ¼ **cup minced fresh parsley**
- 3 **tablespoons 2% milk**
- ¼ **teaspoon salt**
- ⅛ **teaspoon pepper**
- 8 **bacon strips, chopped**
- 2 **medium potatoes, peeled and thinly sliced**
- 2 **green onions, finely chopped**
- 4 **fresh sage leaves, thinly sliced**
- 1 **cup (4 ounces) shredded pepper jack cheese**
- 2 **plum tomatoes, sliced**

1. Preheat oven to 400°. In a large bowl, whisk eggs, parsley, milk, salt and pepper; set aside. In a 10-in. ovenproof skillet, cook bacon over medium heat until partially cooked but not crisp.

2. Add potatoes, onions and sage; cook until potatoes are tender. Reduce heat; sprinkle with cheese. Top with egg mixture and tomato slices.

3. Bake, uncovered, 20-25 minutes or until eggs are completely set. Let stand 15 minutes. Cut into wedges.

AMISH BREAKFAST CASSEROLE

We enjoyed a hearty breakfast bake during a visit to an Amish inn. When I asked for the recipe, one of the women told me the ingredients right off the top of her head. I modified it to create this version my family loves. Breakfast sausage may be used in place of the bacon.

—**BETH NOTARO** KOKOMO, IN

PREP: 15 MIN. • **BAKE:** 35 MIN. + STANDING
MAKES: 12 SERVINGS

- 1 **pound sliced bacon, diced**
- 1 **medium sweet onion, chopped**
- 6 **eggs, lightly beaten**
- 4 **cups frozen shredded hash brown potatoes, thawed**
- 2 **cups (8 ounces) shredded cheddar cheese**
- 1½ **cups (12 ounces) 4% cottage cheese**
- 1¼ **cups shredded Swiss cheese**

1. Preheat oven to 350°. In a large skillet, cook bacon and onion over medium heat until the bacon is crisp; drain. In a large bowl, combine all the remaining ingredients; stir in bacon mixture. Transfer to a greased 13x9-in. baking dish.

2. Bake, uncovered, 35-40 minutes or until a knife inserted near the center comes out clean. Let stand 10 minutes before cutting.

BBQ CHICKEN POLENTA WITH FRIED EGG

In college, BBQ chicken with polenta warmed me up before class. Now I cook it for brunch with friends and family.

—EVAN JANNEY LOS ANGELES, CA

START TO FINISH: 25 MIN.
MAKES: 4 SERVINGS

- 2 **cups shredded cooked chicken breasts**
- ¾ **cup barbecue sauce**
- 1 **tablespoon minced fresh cilantro**
- 2 **tablespoons olive oil, divided**
- 1 **tube (1 pound) polenta, cut into 8 slices**
- 1 **small garlic clove, minced**
- 4 **eggs**

1. In a small saucepan, combine the chicken, barbecue sauce and cilantro; heat through over medium heat, stirring occasionally.

2. In a large skillet, heat 1 tablespoon oil over medium-high heat. Add the polenta; cook 2-3 minutes on each side or until lightly browned. Transfer to a serving plate; keep warm.

3. In same pan, heat remaining oil over medium-high heat. Add garlic; cook and stir 1 minute. Break eggs, one at a time, into pan. Reduce heat to low. Cook until desired doneness, turning after whites are set if desired. Serve over polenta with chicken mixture.

SHREDDED CHICKEN

To make cooked chicken for recipes, simmer boneless chicken breasts in a little water seasoned with salt, pepper and your favorite herbs. Cool and shred or dice, then freeze.

ITALIAN FRITTATA

This recipe has been a longtime family favorite. We love its savory, sweet, subtle Italian flavor. It's colorful, fluffy and a healthy way to start the day.
—**MARLENE KROLL** CHICAGO, IL

START TO FINISH: 25 MIN.
MAKES: 2 SERVINGS

- 1 **package (6 ounces) fresh baby spinach**
- 4 **eggs, lightly beaten**
- 1 **tablespoon diced pimientos, drained**
- 2 **teaspoons Italian seasoning**
- 2 **teaspoons minced fresh parsley or ¾ teaspoon dried parsley flakes**
- 1⅓ **cups sliced fresh mushrooms**
- 4 **green onions, finely chopped**
- 2 **tablespoons butter**
- 2 **teaspoons olive oil**
- 4 **teaspoons grated Parmesan cheese**
  Dash salt

1. In a large saucepan, bring ½ in. of water to a boil. Add spinach; cover and boil 3-5 minutes or until wilted.
2. Meanwhile, in a large bowl, whisk eggs, pimientos, Italian seasoning and parsley; set aside.
3. Drain spinach and pat dry. In a 7-in. ovenproof skillet, saute mushrooms and onions in butter and oil until tender. Reduce heat; sprinkle with spinach, cheese and salt. Top with egg mixture. Cover and cook 4-6 minutes or until nearly set.
4. Uncover skillet. Broil 3-4 in. from heat 2-3 minutes or until eggs are completely set. Let stand 5 minutes before cutting.

EGGS BENEDICT CASSEROLE

Here's a breakfast bake that is as special as eggs Benedict but is great for a crowd.
—**SANDIE HEINDEL** LIBERTY, MO

PREP: 25 MIN. + CHILLING • **BAKE:** 45 MIN.
MAKES: 12 SERVINGS (1⅔ CUPS SAUCE)

- 12 **ounces Canadian bacon, chopped**
- 6 **English muffins, split and cut into 1-inch pieces**
- 8 **eggs**
- 2 **cups 2% milk**
- 1 **teaspoon onion powder**
- ¼ **teaspoon paprika**
  HOLLANDAISE SAUCE
- 4 **egg yolks**
- ½ **cup heavy whipping cream**
- 2 **tablespoons lemon juice**
- 1 **teaspoon Dijon mustard**
- ½ **cup butter, melted**

1. Place half the Canadian bacon in a greased 3-qt. or 13x9-in. baking dish; top with English muffins and remaining bacon. In a large bowl, whisk eggs, milk and onion powder; pour over top. Refrigerate, covered, overnight.
2. Preheat oven to 375°. Remove casserole from refrigerator 30 minutes before baking. Sprinkle with paprika. Bake, covered, 35 minutes. Uncover; bake 10-15 minutes or until a knife inserted near center comes out clean.
3. In top of a double boiler or a metal bowl over simmering water, whisk egg yolks, cream, lemon juice and mustard until blended; cook until mixture is just thick enough to coat a metal spoon and temperature reaches 160°, whisking constantly. Reduce heat to very low. Very slowly drizzle in warm melted butter, whisking constantly. Serve immediately with casserole.

COUNTRY-STYLE SCRAMBLED EGGS

I added a little color and flavor to ordinary scrambled eggs with some green pepper, onion and red potatoes.

—JOYCE PLATFOOT WAPAKONETA, OH

START TO FINISH: 30 MIN.
MAKES: 4 SERVINGS

- 8 **bacon strips, diced**
- 2 **cups diced red potatoes**
- ½ **cup chopped onion**
- ½ **cup chopped green pepper**
- 8 **eggs**
- ¼ **cup milk**
- 1 **teaspoon salt**
- ¼ **teaspoon pepper**
- 1 **cup (4 ounces) shredded cheddar cheese**

1. In a large skillet, cook bacon over medium heat until crisp. Using a slotted spoon, remove to paper towels to drain. Cook and stir potatoes in drippings over medium heat 12 minutes or until potatoes are tender. Add onion and green pepper. Cook and stir 3-4 minutes or until crisp-tender; drain. Stir in the bacon.

2. In a large bowl, whisk the eggs, milk, salt and pepper; add to skillet. Cook and stir until the eggs are completely set. Sprinkle with the cheese and let stand until melted.

Country-Style
Scrambled Eggs

GREEN CHILI BREAKFAST BURRITOS

I lived for a while in the Southwest, where we wrapped everything up in a tortilla. Breakfast burritos in any combination are popular there, especially with green chilies.

—ANGELA SPENGLER MECHANICSBURG, PA

START TO FINISH: 25 MIN.
MAKES: 6 SERVINGS

- 6 **eggs**
- 3 **egg whites**
- 1 **jalapeno pepper, seeded and minced**
  Dash cayenne pepper
- 4 **breakfast turkey sausage links, casings removed**
- ¾ **cup shredded reduced-fat Mexican cheese blend**
- 1 **can (4 ounces) chopped green chilies, drained**
- 6 **whole wheat tortillas (8 inches), warmed**
- 6 **tablespoons salsa**

1. In a small bowl, whisk the eggs, egg whites, jalapeno and cayenne; set aside.

2. Crumble sausage into a large skillet; cook over medium heat until no longer pink. Drain. Push sausage to the sides of pan. Pour egg mixture into center of pan. Cook and stir until set. Sprinkle with cheese and chilies. Remove from the heat; cover and let stand until the cheese is melted.

3. Place ⅓ cup egg mixture off center on each tortilla. Fold sides and end over filling and roll up. Top with salsa.

NOTE *Wear disposable gloves when cutting hot peppers; the oils can burn skin. Avoid touching your face.*

SAUSAGE BREAKFAST HASH

START TO FINISH: 30 MIN.
MAKES: 4 SERVINGS

- 3 tablespoons butter, divided
- 1 package (20 ounces) refrigerated diced potatoes with onion
- 1 package (7 ounces) frozen fully cooked breakfast sausage links, thawed and sliced
- 1 small green pepper, chopped
- 1 small sweet red pepper, chopped
- ¼ teaspoon salt
  Dash cayenne pepper
- 1 cup (4 ounces) shredded Swiss cheese
- 8 eggs
- ¼ teaspoon pepper
  Hot pepper sauce, optional

1. In a large skillet, melt 1 tablespoon butter over medium heat; stir in the potatoes, sausage, green and red peppers, salt and cayenne. Cover and cook 12-14 minutes or until potatoes and vegetables are tender, stirring occasionally. Stir in cheese.
2. In a large skillet, fry eggs in the remaining butter as desired. Sprinkle with pepper. If desired, serve with pepper sauce.

> Served with dough well-done (toast) and dirty water (coffee), this makes a fun breakfast-for-dinner combo.
> —**JACOB KITZMAN** SEATTLE, WA

HAM AND CHEESE MINI STRATAS

Almost too cute to eat, these mini egg bakes make a handy portable meal. Even with a creamy texture, they hold their shape.
—**SHIRLEY WARREN** THIENSVILLE, WI

PREP: 20 MIN. • **BAKE:** 25 MIN.
MAKES: 1 DOZEN

- 1 small onion, chopped
- 1 teaspoon canola oil
- 5 eggs
- 1½ cups 2% milk
- 1 cup (4 ounces) shredded cheddar cheese
- 2 teaspoons Dijon mustard
- ¼ teaspoon salt
- ⅛ teaspoon pepper
- 3 cups cubed day-old Italian bread (½-inch cubes)
- 1 cup cubed fully cooked ham
- 1 plum tomato, seeded and chopped

1. Preheat oven to 350°. In a small skillet, saute onion in oil until tender. In a large bowl, whisk eggs, milk, cheese, mustard, salt and pepper. Stir in bread cubes, ham, tomato and onion.
2. Spoon into greased or foil-lined muffin cups. Bake, uncovered, 22-26 minutes or until a knife inserted near center comes out clean.

BRIE AND PROSCIUTTO TART

Feel free to experiment with this versatile tart. Substitute ham or Canadian bacon for prosciutto and your favorite kind of creamy cheese for Brie.

—AMY TONG ANAHEIM, CA

PREP: 30 MIN. + COOLING • **BAKE:** 30 MIN.
MAKES: 12 SERVINGS

- ½ **cup finely chopped pecans**
- 1½ **cups all-purpose flour**
- 2 **teaspoons sugar**
- ½ **cup cold butter, cubed**
- 1 **egg yolk**
- 1 **tablespoon water**
- 1 **teaspoon Dijon mustard**

FILLING

- 3 **shallots, thinly sliced**
- 1 **tablespoon olive oil**
- 2 **cups fresh baby spinach**
- 4 **thin slices prosciutto or deli ham**
- 3 **eggs**
- ⅔ **cup 2% milk**
- ¼ **teaspoon salt**
- ⅛ **teaspoon pepper**
- ⅛ **teaspoon ground nutmeg**
- ⅛ **teaspoon crushed red pepper flakes**
- 4 **ounces Brie cheese, rind removed and cubed**
- ¼ **teaspoon minced fresh thyme**

1. Preheat oven to 350°. In a food processor, process pecans until finely chopped. Add flour and sugar; cover and pulse until blended. Add butter; cover and pulse until mixture resembles coarse crumbs. In a small bowl, combine egg yolk, water and mustard. While processing, gradually add egg yolk mixture until dough forms a ball.

2. Press onto the bottom and up the sides of an ungreased 14x4-in. fluted tart pan with removable bottom. Bake 18-22 minutes or until crust is lightly browned. Cool on a wire rack.

3. In a large skillet, saute shallots in oil until tender. Add spinach; cook 1-2 minutes longer or until wilted. Remove and set aside to cool.

4. Meanwhile, in the same skillet, cook prosciutto over medium heat until slightly crisp. Remove to paper towels; drain. In a large bowl, whisk eggs, milk and seasonings. Spoon spinach mixture into crust; pour egg mixture over top. Top with prosciutto and cheese.

5. Bake 30-35 minutes or until a knife inserted near center comes out clean. Sprinkle with thyme. Serve warm.

FREEZE OPTION *Before topping with thyme, securely wrap and freeze cooled tart in plastic wrap and foil. To use, partially thaw in refrigerator overnight. Remove from refrigerator 30 minutes before baking. Preheat oven to 350°. Unwrap quiche; reheat in oven until heated through and a thermometer inserted in center reads 165°. Sprinkle with thyme.*

MUSHROOM & ASPARAGUS EGGS BENEDICT

This recipe is easy to make, but it looks as if you spent hours preparing it. I like to serve it with broiled grapefruit topped with brown sugar and ginger for breakfast, and with a mixed green salad tossed with tomatoes and balsamic vinaigrette for brunch.

—NADINE MESCH MOUNT HEALTHY, OH

PREP: 25 MIN. • **COOK:** 25 MIN.
MAKES: 4 SERVINGS

- 12 **fresh asparagus spears**
- 3 **teaspoons olive oil, divided**
- 1 **shallot, finely chopped**
- 2 **tablespoons butter, divided**
- 2⅔ **cups sliced baby portobello mushrooms**
- 2½ **cups sliced fresh shiitake mushrooms**
- 1 **garlic clove, minced**
- ¼ **cup sherry**
- ½ **cup heavy whipping cream**
- ½ **teaspoon salt**
- 1 **tablespoon minced fresh basil**
- 1 **tablespoon white vinegar**
- 4 **eggs**
- 4 **slices French bread (¾ inch thick), toasted**
- ¼ **teaspoon pepper**
- 2 **teaspoons balsamic vinegar**

1. In a large skillet, saute asparagus in 1 teaspoon oil until crisp-tender; remove and keep warm.

2. In same skillet, saute shallot in remaining oil and 1 tablespoon butter until tender. Add mushrooms and garlic; cook 4 minutes longer. Add sherry, stirring to loosen browned bits from pan. Stir in cream and salt. Bring to a boil. Cook and stir 1-2 minutes or until slightly thickened. Stir in basil.

3. Meanwhile, place 2-3 in. of water in a large skillet with high sides; add white vinegar. Bring to a boil; reduce heat and simmer gently. Break cold eggs, one at a time, into a custard cup or saucer; holding the cup close to the surface of the water, slip each egg into water.

4. Cook, uncovered, until whites are completely set and yolks are still soft, about 4 minutes. With a slotted spoon, lift eggs out of the water.

5. Spread remaining butter over toast slices. Top each with asparagus, a poached egg and mushroom mixture. Sprinkle with pepper and drizzle with balsamic vinegar. Serve immediately.

BRUNCH NOTES

_____   _____
_____   _____
_____   _____
_____   _____
_____   _____
_____   _____
_____   _____

Italian Sausage
Quiche

ITALIAN SAUSAGE QUICHE

This—our most popular recipe—is prepared with mild Italian sausage made especially for us by our local butcher. For the best flavor, use a mildly spiced sausage.
—**LEE ANN MILLER** MILLERSBURG, OH

PREP: 30 MIN. • **BAKE:** 35 MIN. + STANDING
MAKES: 6 SERVINGS

> Pastry for single-crust pie
> (9 inches)
> 1 **pound bulk Italian sausage**
> ¼ **cup chopped onion**
> ¼ **cup chopped green pepper**
> 4 **teaspoons chopped seeded
> jalapeno pepper**
> 1 **cup (4 ounces) shredded sharp
> cheddar cheese**
> 3 **eggs**
> 1 **cup heavy whipping cream**
> 1 **teaspoon minced fresh parsley**
> 1 **teaspoon minced fresh basil**
> ¼ **teaspoon pepper**
> ⅛ **teaspoon salt**
> **Dash garlic powder**
> **Dash cayenne pepper**

1. Preheat oven to 450°. Roll out pastry to fit a 9-in. pie plate. Transfer pastry to pie plate. Trim pastry to ½ in. beyond edge of plate; flute edges. Line unpricked pastry with a double thickness of heavy-duty foil. Fill with dried beans, uncooked rice or pie weights.
2. Bake 8 minutes. Remove foil and weights; bake 5 minutes longer. Cool on a wire rack. Reduce oven setting to 375°.
3. Meanwhile, in a large skillet, cook sausage, onion, green pepper and jalapeno over medium heat until meat is no longer pink; drain. Spoon into shell and sprinkle with cheese.

4. In a large bowl, whisk remaining ingredients; pour over cheese. Bake 35-40 minutes or until a knife inserted near center comes out clean. Let stand 10 minutes before cutting.
NOTE *Wear disposable gloves when cutting hot peppers; the oils can burn skin. Avoid touching your face.*

BREAKFAST SPUDS

Here's a dish that has it all—sweet potatoes, eggs, ham and cheese—for a powerful start to the day.
—**ANNIE RUNDLE** MUSKEGO, WI

START TO FINISH: 30 MIN.
MAKES: 6 SERVINGS

> 1 **package (20 ounces) frozen sweet
> potato puffs**
> 8 **eggs**
> ⅓ **cup 2% milk**
> ¼ **teaspoon salt**
> ⅛ **teaspoon pepper**
> 1 **cup cubed fully cooked ham**
> 1 **tablespoon butter**
> **Shredded cheddar cheese and
> sliced green onions**

1. Bake potato puffs according to package directions. In a large bowl, whisk eggs, milk, salt and pepper. Stir in ham.
2. In a large nonstick skillet, heat butter over medium heat. Add egg mixture; cook and stir until eggs are thickened and no liquid egg remains. Serve with potato puffs; sprinkle with cheese and green onions.

HAM & CHEESE BREAKFAST STRUDELS

Golden breakfast strudels are guaranteed to get the morning off to a terrific start. Sometimes I assemble them ahead and freeze them individually before baking.

—JO GROTH PLAINFIELD, IA

PREP: 25 MIN. • **BAKE:** 10 MIN.
MAKES: 6 SERVINGS

- 3 **tablespoons butter, divided**
- 2 **tablespoons all-purpose flour**
- 1 **cup milk**
- ⅓ **cup shredded Swiss cheese**
- 2 **tablespoons grated Parmesan cheese**
- ¼ **teaspoon salt**
- 5 **eggs, lightly beaten**
- ¼ **pound ground fully cooked ham (about ¾ cup)**
- 6 **sheets phyllo dough (14x9 inch)**
- ½ **cup butter, melted**
- ¼ **cup dry bread crumbs**

TOPPING

- 2 **tablespoons grated Parmesan cheese**
- 2 **tablespoons minced fresh parsley**

1. In a saucepan, melt 2 tablespoons butter. Stir in flour until smooth; gradually add milk. Bring to a boil; cook and stir 2 minutes or until thickened. Stir in cheeses and salt.

2. In a large nonstick skillet, melt remaining butter over medium heat. Add eggs; cook and stir until almost set. Stir in ham and cheese sauce; heat through. Remove from heat.

3. Preheat oven to 375°. Place one sheet of phyllo dough on a work surface. (Keep remaining phyllo covered with plastic wrap and a damp towel to prevent it from drying out.) Brush with melted butter. Sprinkle with 2 teaspoons bread crumbs. Fold in half lengthwise; brush again with butter. Spoon ½ cup filling onto phyllo about 2 in. from a short side. Fold side and edges over filling and roll up. Brush with butter. Repeat with remaining sheets of phyllo, butter, bread crumbs and filling.

4. Place on a greased baking sheet; sprinkle each with 1 teaspoon cheese and 1 teaspoon parsley. Bake 10-15 minutes or until golden brown. Serve immediately.

USING PHYLLO

Handling the thin, fragile sheets of phyllo quickly is a key to success. Count out the number of phyllo sheets required for the recipe. Place the sheets on a smooth, dry surface and immediately cover as recipe directs. Gently pull sheets from the stack as you need them, keeping the remaining sheets covered until needed.

BLT EGG BAKE

BLT's are a favorite at my house, so I created this casserole to combine those flavors in a fancier dish. It was such a hit, I served it to my church ladies group at a brunch I hosted. I received lots of compliments and wrote out the recipe many times that day.

—PRISCILLA DETRICK CATOOSA, OK

START TO FINISH: 30 MIN.
MAKES: 4 SERVINGS

- ¼ cup mayonnaise
- 5 slices bread, toasted
- 4 slices process American cheese
- 12 bacon strips, cooked and crumbled
- 4 eggs
- 1 medium tomato, halved and sliced
- 2 tablespoons butter
- 2 tablespoons all-purpose flour
- ¼ teaspoon salt
- ⅛ teaspoon pepper
- 1 cup 2% milk
- ½ cup shredded cheddar cheese
- 2 green onions, thinly sliced
  Shredded lettuce

1. Preheat oven to 325°. Spread the mayonnaise on one side of each slice of toast and cut into small pieces. Arrange toast, mayonnaise side up, in a greased 8-in.-square baking dish. Top with cheese slices and bacon.

2. In a large skillet, fry eggs over medium heat until completely set; place over bacon. Top with tomato slices; set aside.

3. In a small saucepan, melt butter. Stir in flour, salt and pepper until smooth. Gradually add milk. Bring to a boil; cook and stir 2 minutes or until thickened.

4. Pour over the tomatoes. Sprinkle with the cheddar cheese and onions. Bake, uncovered, 10 minutes. Cut into squares; serve with lettuce.

FARM FRESH QUICHE

Going to the farmers market and talking with people who work on the farm inspires me to make recipes like this one, a quiche loaded with veggies.

—**HEATHER KING** FROSTBURG, MD

PREP: 35 MIN. • **BAKE:** 30 MIN. + STANDING
MAKES: 6 SERVINGS

- ¼ **cup olive oil**
- 1 **bunch broccoli, cut into florets**
- 1 **small onion, finely chopped**
- 3 **cups chopped fresh mustard greens or spinach**
- 3 **garlic cloves, minced**
- 1 **sheet refrigerated pie pastry**
- 4 **eggs**
- 1 **cup 2% milk**
- 1 **tablespoon minced fresh rosemary or 1 teaspoon dried rosemary, crushed**
- ½ **teaspoon salt**
- ½ **teaspoon pepper**
- ½ **cup shredded smoked cheddar cheese, divided**
- ½ **cup shredded Swiss cheese, divided**

1. Preheat oven to 375°. In a large skillet, heat oil over medium-high heat. Add broccoli and onion; cook and stir until broccoli is crisp-tender. Stir in greens and garlic; cook and stir 4-5 minutes longer or until greens are wilted.

2. Unroll pastry sheet into a 9-in. pie plate; flute edge. Fill with broccoli mixture. In a small bowl, whisk eggs, milk, rosemary, salt and pepper. Stir in ¼ cup cheddar cheese and ¼ cup Swiss cheese; pour over vegetables. Sprinkle with remaining cheeses.

3. Bake 30-35 minutes or until a knife inserted near center comes out clean. Let stand 15 minutes before cutting.

SWEET ORANGE CROISSANT PUDDING

Time-crunched cooks are sure to welcome the make-ahead convenience of my delightful dish. Feel free to replace the orange marmalade with any jam or jelly that suits your taste.

—**MARY GABRIEL** LAS VEGAS, NV

PREP: 15 MIN. + CHILLING
BAKE: 40 MIN. + COOLING
MAKES: 8 SERVINGS

- 4 **croissants, split**
- 1 **cup orange marmalade, divided**
- 3 **eggs**
- 1¼ **cups milk**
- 1 **cup heavy whipping cream**
- ½ **cup sugar**
- 1 **teaspoon grated orange peel, optional**
- ½ **teaspoon almond extract**

1. Spread croissant bottoms with 3 tablespoons marmalade; replace tops. Cut each croissant into five slices; place in a greased 11x7-in. baking dish.
2. In a large bowl, whisk eggs, milk, cream, sugar, orange peel if desired and extract; pour over croissants. Cover and refrigerate overnight.
3. Remove from the refrigerator 30 minutes before baking. Preheat oven to 350°. Place dish in a larger baking dish. Fill larger dish with 1 in. of boiling water.
4. Bake, uncovered, 40-45 minutes or until a knife inserted near center comes out clean.
5. Remove pan from water bath; cool on a wire rack 10 minutes. Brush remaining marmalade over the top. Cut and serve warm.

BREAKFAST CUSTARD

With a side of warmed ham and whole wheat toast, this custard makes for a satisfying breakfast.

—**ARLENE BENDER** MARTIN, ND

START TO FINISH: 25 MIN.
MAKES: 4 SERVINGS

- 4 **eggs, lightly beaten**
- 2 **tablespoons butter, melted**
- 1 **cup milk**
- 1 **teaspoon cornstarch**
- ⅛ **teaspoon baking powder**
- ¼ **teaspoon salt**
  Dash pepper
- ½ **cup shredded cheddar cheese**

1. Preheat oven to 425°. In a large bowl, whisk the first seven ingredients. Stir in cheese. Pour into four buttered 4-oz. custard cups.
2. Place cups in a baking pan. Fill pan with boiling water to a depth of 1 in. Bake, uncovered, 15-20 minutes or until a knife inserted near the center comes out clean.

BRUNCH NOTES

SPINACH HASH BROWN FRITTATA

I love this frittata! Not only does it have eggs, bacon and potatoes, it has spinach and lots of gooey cheese.

—GILDA LESTER MILLSBORO, DE

PREP: 25 MIN. • **BAKE:** 35 MIN. + STANDING
MAKES: 8 SERVINGS

- 1 large onion, finely chopped
- 1 tablespoon olive oil
- 2 garlic cloves, minced
- 1 package (10 ounces) frozen chopped spinach, thawed and squeezed dry
- ¼ teaspoon salt
- ¼ teaspoon pepper
- 2 ounces pancetta or bacon strips, finely chopped
- 3 cups frozen shredded hash brown potatoes, thawed
- 8 eggs, lightly beaten
- 1 cup 2% milk
- 1 cup (4 ounces) fontina cheese, divided
- 1 cup (4 ounces) shredded cheddar cheese, divided
- ¼ cup minced fresh parsley
- 1 tablespoon Worcestershire sauce
- 1 teaspoon ground mustard
- ¼ teaspoon ground nutmeg

1. Preheat oven to 350°. In a large skillet, saute onion in oil until tender. Add garlic; cook 1 minute longer. Stir in the spinach, salt and pepper. Remove from heat.

2. In another skillet, cook pancetta over medium heat until crisp. Remove pancetta to paper towels with a slotted spoon; drain.

3. In a greased 11x7-in. baking dish, layer hash browns, spinach mixture and pancetta. In a bowl, whisk eggs, milk, ½ cup fontina cheese, ½ cup cheddar cheese, parsley, Worcestershire sauce, mustard and nutmeg; pour over top. Sprinkle with remaining cheeses.

4. Bake, uncovered, 35-40 minutes or until a knife inserted near the center comes out clean. Let stand 10 minutes before cutting.

EASY BREAKFAST STRATA

Starting this breakfast casserole at night has two advantages: Not only is it ready for the oven when I get up, and I don't have to deal with dirty dishes first thing in the morning!

—DEBBIE JOHNSON CENTERTOWN, MO

PREP: 20 MIN. + CHILLING • **BAKE:** 30 MIN.
MAKES: 12 SERVINGS

- 1 pound bulk pork sausage
- 1 large green pepper, chopped
- 1 medium onion, chopped
- 1 loaf (1 pound) herb or cheese bakery bread, cubed
- 1 cup (4 ounces) shredded cheddar cheese
- 6 eggs
- 2 cups 2% milk
- 1 teaspoon ground mustard

1. In a large skillet, cook the sausage, pepper and onion over medium heat until meat is no longer pink; drain.

2. Place bread in a greased 13x9-in. baking dish. Top with sausage; sprinkle with cheese. In a large bowl, whisk eggs, milk and mustard. Pour over top. Cover and refrigerate overnight.

3. Remove from the refrigerator 30 minutes before baking. Preheat oven to 350°. Bake, uncovered, 30-35 minutes or until a knife inserted near center comes out clean. Let stand 5 minutes before cutting.

Easy Breakfast
Strata

SPIRAL OMELET SUPREME

You can substitute 2 cups of any combination of your favorite omelet fillings for the vegetables in this recipe. A serrated knife works well for slicing it.

—**DEBBIE MORRIS** HAMILTON, OH

PREP: 20 MIN. • **BAKE:** 20 MIN.
MAKES: 8 SERVINGS

- 4 **ounces cream cheese, softened**
- ¾ **cup 2% milk**
- ¼ **cup plus 2 tablespoons grated Parmesan cheese, divided**
- 2 **tablespoons all-purpose flour**
- 12 **eggs**
- 1 **large green pepper, chopped**
- 1 **cup sliced fresh mushrooms**
- 1 **small onion, chopped**
- 2 **teaspoons canola oil**
- 1½ **cups (6 ounces) shredded part-skim mozzarella cheese**
- 1 **plum tomato, seeded and chopped**
- 1¼ **teaspoons Italian seasoning, divided**

1. Preheat oven to 375°. Line the bottom and sides of a greased 15x10x 1-in. baking pan with parchment paper; grease the paper and set aside.
2. In a small bowl, beat cream cheese and milk until smooth. Beat in ¼ cup Parmesan cheese and flour until blended. In a large bowl, beat eggs; add cream cheese mixture and mix well. Pour into prepared pan. Bake 20-25 minutes or until set.
3. Meanwhile, in a large skillet, saute the pepper, mushrooms and onion in oil until crisp-tender. Keep warm.
4. Turn omelet onto a work surface; peel off parchment paper. Sprinkle with the vegetable mixture, mozzarella cheese, tomato and 1 teaspoon Italian seasoning. Roll up jelly-roll style, starting with a short side. Place on a serving platter. Sprinkle with remaining Parmesan cheese and Italian seasoning.

SOUTHWEST TORTILLA SCRAMBLE

Here's my version of a deconstructed breakfast burrito that's actually good for you. Go for hefty corn tortillas in this recipe. Flour ones can get lost in the scramble.

—**CHRISTINE SCHENHER** EXETER, CA

START TO FINISH: 15 MIN.
MAKES: 2 SERVINGS

- 4 **egg whites**
- 2 **eggs**
- ¼ **teaspoon pepper**
- 2 **corn tortillas (6 inches), halved and cut into strips**
- ¼ **cup chopped fresh spinach**
- 2 **tablespoons shredded reduced-fat cheddar cheese**
- ¼ **cup salsa**

1. In a large bowl, whisk egg whites, eggs and pepper. Stir in the tortillas, spinach and cheese.
2. Heat a large skillet coated with cooking spray over medium heat. Pour in egg mixture; cook and stir until the eggs are thickened and no liquid egg remains. Stir in salsa.

ITALIAN PIZZA OMELET

Savory and special, this tasty omelet with classic pizza flavors will be a hit with all who taste it.

—AGNES WARD STRATFORD, ON

START TO FINISH: 20 MIN.
MAKES: 1 SERVING

- ¾ **cup sliced fresh mushrooms**
- 2 **tablespoons chopped onion**
- 2 **teaspoons olive oil**
- 1 **tablespoon butter**
- 3 **eggs**
- 3 **tablespoons water**
- ⅛ **teaspoon salt**
- ⅛ **teaspoon pepper**
- ¼ **cup shredded part-skim mozzarella cheese**
- ¼ **cup marinara sauce or spaghetti sauce, warmed**

1. In a small nonstick skillet, saute mushrooms and onion in oil until tender. Remove from skillet and set aside.

2. In the same skillet, melt butter over medium-high heat. Whisk the eggs, water, salt and pepper. Add the egg mixture to the skillet (mixture should set immediately at edges).

3. As eggs set, push cooked edges toward the center, letting uncooked portion flow underneath. When the eggs are set, spoon mushroom mixture on one side and sprinkle with cheese; fold other side over filling. Slide omelet onto a plate. Serve with marinara sauce.

ASPARAGUS PHYLLO BAKE

I'm Greek and I grew up wrapping lots of foods in phyllo. During asparagus season, I bring out the phyllo and start baking.

—BONNIE GEAVARAS-BOOTZ
SCOTTSDALE, AZ

PREP: 25 MIN. • **BAKE:** 50 MIN.
MAKES: 12 SERVINGS

- 2 **pounds fresh asparagus, trimmed and cut into 1-inch pieces**
- 5 **eggs, lightly beaten**
- 1 **carton (15 ounces) ricotta cheese**
- 1 **cup (4 ounces) shredded Swiss cheese**
- 2 **tablespoons grated Parmesan cheese**
- 2 **garlic cloves, minced**
- ½ **teaspoon salt**
- ½ **teaspoon grated lemon peel**
- ½ **teaspoon pepper**
- ½ **cup slivered almonds, toasted**
- ¾ **cup butter, melted**
- 16 **sheets phyllo dough (14x9 inches)**

1. In a large saucepan, bring 8 cups water to a boil. Add asparagus; cook, uncovered, 30 seconds or just until asparagus turns bright green. Remove asparagus and immediately drop into ice water. Drain and pat dry. In a large bowl, mix eggs, cheeses and seasonings; stir in almonds and asparagus.

2. Preheat oven to 375°. Brush a 13x9-in. baking dish with some of the butter. Unroll phyllo dough. Layer eight sheets of phyllo in prepared dish, brushing each with butter. (Keep remaining phyllo covered with plastic wrap and a damp towel to prevent it from drying out.)

3. Spread ricotta mixture over phyllo layers. Top with remaining phyllo sheets, brushing each with butter. Cut into 12 rectangles. Bake 50-55 minutes or until golden brown.

NOTE *To toast nuts, spread in a dry nonstick skillet and heat over low heat until lightly browned; stir occasionally.*

HAM VEGETABLE STRATA

PREP: 20 MIN. + CHILLING
BAKE: 50 MIN. + STANDING
MAKES: 12-16 SERVINGS

- 1 **small zucchini, cut into ¼-inch slices**
- 2 **cups fresh broccoli florets**
- ½ **cup shredded carrot**
- 12 **slices white bread, crusts removed**
- 1 **cup cubed fully cooked ham**
- 1 **can (8 ounces) mushroom stems and pieces, drained**
- 1 **cup (4 ounces) shredded sharp cheddar cheese**
- 1 **cup (4 ounces) shredded Swiss cheese**
- 12 **eggs**
- 2½ **cups milk**
- ¼ **cup chopped onion**
- ½ **teaspoon ground mustard**
- ¼ **teaspoon salt**
- ⅛ **teaspoon pepper**
- 1½ **cups crushed cornflakes**
- ¼ **cup butter, melted**

1. Place 1 in. water in a small saucepan. Add zucchini, broccoli and carrot. Cook 5-10 minutes or until tender; drain.

2. Meanwhile, cut each bread slice in half diagonally; place half of the pieces in a greased 13x9-in. baking dish. Top with half of the vegetables, ham, mushrooms and cheeses. Repeat layers. In a large bowl, whisk the eggs, milk, onion, mustard, salt and pepper; pour over the ham mixture. Cover and refrigerate for 8 hours or overnight.

3. Remove from the refrigerator 30 minutes before baking. Toss cornflakes and butter; sprinkle over the casserole. Preheat oven to 350°. Bake, uncovered, 50-60 minutes or until a knife inserted near the center comes out clean. Let stand 10 minutes before cutting.

> Ever since my niece gave me this recipe, I've shared it with many of my friends. The crunchy, golden brown topping and colorful ingredients present a tantalizing dish. It's my favorite brunch entree to serve.
>
> —**DIANE MEYER** GENESEO, NY

BRUNCH NOTES

_____   _____
_____   _____
_____   _____
_____   _____
_____   _____
_____   _____

SOUTHWEST HASH WITH ADOBO-LIME CREMA

PREP: 20 MIN. • **BAKE:** 25 MIN.
MAKES: 4 SERVINGS

- 3 **medium sweet potatoes (about 1½ pounds), cubed**
- 1 **medium onion, chopped**
- 1 **medium sweet red pepper, chopped**
- 1 **tablespoon canola oil**
- 1 **teaspoon garlic powder**
- 1 **teaspoon smoked paprika**
- ¾ **teaspoon ground chipotle pepper**
- ½ **teaspoon salt**
- ¼ **teaspoon pepper**
- ⅔ **cup canned black beans, rinsed and drained**
- 4 **eggs**
- ½ **cup reduced-fat sour cream**
- 2 **tablespoons lime juice**
- 2 **teaspoons adobo sauce**
- ½ **medium ripe avocado, peeled and sliced, optional**
- 2 **tablespoons minced fresh cilantro**

1. Preheat oven to 400°. Place sweet potatoes, onion and red pepper in a 15x10x1-in. baking pan coated with cooking spray. Drizzle with oil; sprinkle with seasonings. Toss to coat. Roast 25-30 minutes or until potatoes are tender, adding beans during the last 10 minutes of cooking time.

2. Place 2-3 in. of water in a large saucepan or skillet with high sides. Bring to a boil; adjust heat to maintain a gentle simmer. Break cold eggs, one at a time, into a small bowl; holding bowl close to surface of water, slip the egg into water.

3. Cook, uncovered, 3-5 minutes or until whites are completely set and yolks begin to thicken but are not hard. Using a slotted spoon, lift the eggs out of the water.

4. In a small bowl, mix sour cream, lime juice and adobo sauce. Serve sweet potato mixture with egg, sour cream mixture and, if desired, avocado. Sprinkle with cilantro.

Add a splash of white vinegar to the poaching water right before you drop in the eggs. It helps keep them from separating. If you have leftover pulled pork, toss it into the hash for some serious yum.

—**BROOKE KELLER** LEXINGTON, KY

CANADIAN BACON ONION QUICHE

For over 20 years, we sold our homegrown specialty onions at the farmers market. I handed out this favorite recipe for a classic quiche to all our customers.

—JANICE REDFORD CAMBRIDGE, WI

PREP: 30 MIN. • **BAKE:** 40 MIN.
MAKES: 6-8 SERVINGS

- 1 **cup all-purpose flour**
- ¾ **teaspoon salt, divided**
- ½ **cup plus 3 tablespoons cold butter, divided**
- ½ **cup 4% small-curd cottage cheese**
- 3 **large sweet onions, sliced (about 6 cups)**
- 4 **ounces Canadian bacon, diced**
- ¼ **teaspoon pepper**
- 3 **eggs, lightly beaten**
- 1 **cup (4 ounces) shredded cheddar cheese**

1. Preheat oven to 350°. In a small bowl, combine flour and ¼ teaspoon salt; cut in ½ cup butter until crumbly. Gradually add cottage cheese, tossing with a fork until dough forms a ball.

2. Roll out pastry to fit a 9-in. pie plate. Transfer pastry to the pie plate. Trim pastry to ½ in. beyond edge of plate; flute edges.

3. In a large skillet, saute onions in remaining butter until golden brown. Stir in Canadian bacon, pepper and remaining salt. Remove from heat; add eggs and cheddar cheese. Pour into pastry shell.

4. Bake 40-45 minutes or until a knife inserted near center comes out clean.

Broccoli Quiche
Crepe Cups

BROCCOLI QUICHE CREPE CUPS

When I was young and just learning to cook, this was one of the first recipes I made—and I still make it.
—**KRISTIN ARNETT** ELKHORN, WI

PREP: 40 MIN. + CHILLING • **BAKE:** 30 MIN.
MAKES: 4 SERVINGS

1½ **cups milk**
3 **eggs**
1 **cup all-purpose flour**
¼ **teaspoon salt**

FILLING

1 **package (10 ounces) frozen broccoli with cheese sauce**
3 **bacon strips, diced**
½ **cup chopped onion**
2 **eggs**
¼ **cup milk**

1. In a blender, cover and process the first four ingredients until smooth. Cover and chill 1 hour.

2. Heat a lightly greased 8-in. nonstick skillet over medium heat; pour 2 tablespoons batter into center of skillet. Lift and tilt pan to coat bottom evenly. Cook until top appears dry; turn and cook 15-20 seconds longer. Remove to a wire rack. Repeat with remaining batter, greasing skillet as needed. When cool, stack crepes with waxed paper or paper towels in between.

3. Preheat oven to 350°. Line each of four 6-oz. custard cups with a crepe; set aside. Freeze remaining crepes in a freezer bag, leaving waxed paper between each crepe, up to 3 months.

4. For filling, cook broccoli according to package directions. Cut up any larger pieces of broccoli. In a microwave-safe bowl, microwave bacon on high 2 minutes; drain. Add onion; microwave on high 3 minutes or until tender. Beat eggs and milk; stir in broccoli mixture and bacon mixture. Spoon into prepared crepe cups.

5. Bake, uncovered, 30-35 minutes or until a knife inserted near center comes out clean. Remove from the custard cups and serve immediately.

HERB & VEGGIE BRUNCH FRITTATA

A friend called and asked me for a special recipe that could be served at his daughter's wedding brunch, so I created this recipe for the occasion. Loaded with bright veggies, it looks beautiful on a buffet.

—KRISTIN ARNETT ELKHORN, WI

PREP: 15 MIN. • **BAKE:** 55 MIN. + STANDING
MAKES: 12-15 SERVINGS

- 1 pound fresh asparagus, trimmed and cut into 1-inch pieces
- ½ pound sliced fresh mushrooms
- 1 medium sweet red pepper, diced
- 1 medium sweet yellow pepper, diced
- 1 small onion, chopped
- 3 green onions, chopped
- 3 tablespoons olive oil
- 2 garlic cloves, minced
- 3 plum tomatoes, seeded and chopped
- 14 eggs, lightly beaten
- 2 cups half-and-half cream
- 2 cups (8 ounces) shredded Colby-Monterey Jack cheese
- 3 tablespoons minced fresh parsley
- 3 tablespoons minced fresh basil
- ½ teaspoon salt
- ¼ teaspoon pepper
- ½ cup shredded Parmesan cheese

1. Preheat oven to 350°. In a large skillet, saute asparagus, mushrooms, peppers and onions in oil until tender. Add garlic; cook 1 minute longer. Add tomatoes; set aside.

2. In a large bowl, whisk eggs, cream, Colby-Monterey Jack cheese, parsley, basil, salt and pepper; stir into the vegetable mixture.

3. Pour into a greased 13x9-in. baking dish. Bake, uncovered, 45 minutes.

4. Sprinkle with Parmesan cheese. Bake 10-15 minutes longer or until a knife inserted near the center comes out clean. Let frittata stand 10 minutes before cutting.

COLORFUL CHEESE OMELET

When I start my day with this omelet, I can go nonstop, and I know I'm getting valuable nutrients besides.

—LYNDA O'DELL LYNCH PORT HURON, MI

START TO FINISH: 20 MIN.
MAKES: 1 SERVING

- 1 egg
- 2 egg whites
- 2 tablespoons chopped fresh baby spinach
- ⅛ teaspoon hot pepper sauce
- 2 tablespoons chopped sweet red pepper
- 1 green onion, chopped
- 2 tablespoons shredded cheddar cheese

1. In a small bowl, whisk the egg, egg whites, spinach and pepper sauce; set aside. In a small nonstick skillet coated with cooking spray, saute red pepper and onion until tender. Reduce heat to medium.

2. Add egg mixture to skillet (mixture should set immediately at edges). As eggs set, push cooked edges toward the center, letting uncooked portion flow underneath. When the eggs are set, sprinkle with cheese; fold omelet in half. Slide omelet onto a plate.

TURKEY SWISS QUICHE

This quiche is the perfect solution to what to do with leftover turkey. My family looks forward to it every year after Thanksgiving.
—**LOIS FOREHAND**
LITTLE RIVER-ACADEMY, TX

PREP: 25 MIN. • **BAKE:** 30 MIN. + STANDING
MAKES: 6 SERVINGS

- 1 **unbaked pastry shell (9 inches)**
- 1½ **cups finely chopped cooked turkey**
- 4 **eggs**
- ¾ **cup half-and-half cream**
- 2 **cups (8 ounces) shredded Swiss cheese**
- 4 **green onions, finely chopped**
- 2 **tablespoons diced pimientos**
- 1 **teaspoon dried oregano**
- 1 **teaspoon dried parsley flakes**
  Dash salt and pepper
- 3 **slices (¾ ounce each) Swiss cheese, cut into thin strips**

1. Preheat oven to 450°. Line unpricked pastry shell with a double thickness of heavy-duty foil. Bake 8 minutes. Remove foil; bake 5-7 minutes longer or until golden brown. Reduce oven setting to 375°.

2. Sprinkle turkey into pastry shell. In a large bowl, whisk eggs and cream. Stir in the shredded Swiss cheese, onions, pimientos, oregano, parsley, salt and pepper. Pour into crust.

3. Bake 20 minutes. Arrange the Swiss cheese strips in a lattice pattern over the quiche. Bake 10-15 minutes longer or until a knife inserted near center comes out clean. Let stand 10 minutes before cutting.

QUICHE PASTRY CUPS

My grandmother used to make "egg cup surprises" for family brunches on special occasions. The added fillings were always a surprise because she never seemed to use the same combination of ingredients twice. As children, we had a guessing game as to what we'd find in the tender crust, which added an aspect of fun to our meal.

—DENALEE STANDART RANCHO MURETA, CA

PREP: 30 MIN. • **BAKE:** 15 MIN.
MAKES: 1½ DOZEN

- 1 **package (17.3 ounces) frozen puff pastry, thawed**
- 4 **eggs**
- 1 **cup plus 2 tablespoons half-and-half cream, divided**
- 1 **tablespoon minced fresh thyme**
- ½ **teaspoon salt**
- ½ **teaspoon pepper**
- ¼ **teaspoon ground nutmeg**
- 1½ **cups (6 ounces) shredded Gruyere cheese**
- 1½ **cups chopped fresh spinach**
- 1 **medium sweet red pepper, chopped**
- 8 **bacon strips, cooked and crumbled**

1. Preheat oven to 400°. On a lightly floured surface, unfold puff pastry. Roll each sheet into a 12-in. square; cut each into nine squares. Place each square into an ungreased muffin cup, pressing gently onto bottom and up side, allowing corners to point up.
2. In a small bowl, whisk 3 eggs, 1 cup cream, thyme and the seasonings. In another bowl, combine cheese, spinach, red pepper and bacon; divide among pastry cups. Pour egg mixture over cheese mixture.
3. In a small bowl, whisk remaining egg with remaining cream; brush over pastry edges. Bake 15-18 minutes or until golden brown. Remove to wire racks. Serve warm.

JACK CHEESE OVEN OMELET

Although it's easy, this omelet looks impressive. Sometimes I toss in mushrooms and cheddar cheese for a different flavor.

—LAUREL ROBERTS VANCOUVER, WA

PREP: 20 MIN. • **BAKE:** 35 MIN.
MAKES: 6 SERVINGS

- 8 **bacon strips, diced**
- 4 **green onions, sliced**
- 8 **eggs**
- 1 **cup 2% milk**
- ½ **teaspoon seasoned salt**
- 2½ **cups (10 ounces) shredded Monterey Jack cheese, divided**

1. Preheat oven to 350°. In a skillet, cook bacon over medium heat until crisp. Drain skillet; reserve 1 tablespoon drippings. Set bacon aside. Saute onions in drippings until tender; set aside.
2. In a large bowl, beat eggs. Add milk, seasoned salt, 2 cups cheese, bacon and sauteed onions. Transfer to a greased shallow 2-qt. baking dish.
3. Bake, uncovered, 35-40 minutes or until eggs are set. Sprinkle with the remaining cheese.

EGG DATES

According to the American Egg Board, eggs can be used up to 5 weeks after the date printed on the carton. The date on the carton is actually the last day the eggs can be sold.

Quiche
Pastry Cups

PROSCIUTTO & CHEDDAR BREAKFAST BISCUITS

When my family visits, I love to make my nephew happy by making breakfast with pork and cheese. I created this as a twist on the traditional breakfast sandwich for him.

—KELLY BOE WHITELAND, IN

PREP: 30 MIN. • **BAKE:** 15 MIN.
MAKES: 6 SERVINGS

- 2⅓ cups biscuit/baking mix
- ½ cup 2% milk
- 3 tablespoons butter, melted
- 1 to 2 tablespoons minced fresh chives

EGGS

- 6 eggs
- 2 tablespoons 2% milk
- ¼ teaspoon salt
- 2 ounces thinly sliced prosciutto or deli ham, cut into strips
- 2 green onions, chopped
- 1 tablespoon butter
- ½ cup shredded cheddar cheese

1. Preheat oven to 425°. In a bowl, mix biscuit mix, milk, melted butter and chives; mix just until moistened.

2. Turn onto a lightly floured surface; knead gently 8-10 times. Pat or roll to ¾-in. thickness; cut with a floured 2½-in. biscuit cutter. Place 2 in. apart on an ungreased baking sheet. Bake 12-14 minutes or until golden brown.

3. Meanwhile, in a large bowl, whisk eggs, milk and salt. Place a large skillet over medium heat. Add prosciutto and green onions; cook until prosciutto begins to brown, stirring occasionally. Stir in butter until melted. Add egg mixture; cook and stir until eggs are thickened and no liquid egg remains. Stir in cheese; remove from heat.

4. Split warm biscuits in half. Fill with egg mixture.

SUNNY-SIDE-UP HERBED TART

Feel free to be creative with this versatile egg tart. Try Canadian bacon or ham as the meat ingredient, and add toppings such as thyme, chopped spinach or goat cheese.

—DIANA NEVES LAFAYETTE, CA

PREP: 30 MIN. • **BAKE:** 20 MIN.
MAKES: 4 SERVINGS

- 4 **slices pancetta or 4 bacon strips**
- 1 **cup sliced fresh mushrooms**
- 2 **tablespoons chopped shallot**
- 1 **tablespoon olive oil**
- 1 **tablespoon minced fresh tarragon or 1 teaspoon dried tarragon**
- 1 **teaspoon sherry, optional**
- ¼ **cup shredded Gruyere or Swiss cheese**
- ¼ **cup shredded cheddar cheese**
- 3 **tablespoons sour cream**
- ⅛ **teaspoon salt**
  Dash pepper

TART
- 1 **sheet frozen puff pastry, thawed**
- 5 **eggs**
- 1 **teaspoon water**
- 1 **tablespoon minced chives**
  Dash each salt and pepper

1. Preheat oven to 425°. In a large skillet, cook pancetta over medium heat until partially cooked but not crisp. Remove to paper towels to drain. In a small skillet, saute the mushrooms and shallot in oil until tender. Add the tarragon and, if desired, sherry; cook 1 minute longer.

2. Remove from heat; stir in cheeses, sour cream, salt and pepper. Set aside.

3. On a lightly floured surface, unfold the puff pastry. Roll into a 10x9-in. rectangle. Transfer to a 15x10x1-in. parchment paper-lined baking sheet. Prick with a fork.

4. Spread mushroom mixture over pastry to within 1 in. of edges. Top with pancetta (place pancetta near the edges of the mushroom mixture). Score edges of pastry with a fork. Beat 1 egg and water; brush over the pastry edges. Bake 10-12 minutes or until the pastry is golden brown.

5. Carefully crack the remaining eggs, placing off-center on each corner. Bake 8-10 minutes longer or until the eggs are set. Sprinkle with the chives, salt and pepper. Cut into four pieces. Serve warm.

BRUNCH NOTES

BRUNCH NOTES

_____
_____
_____
_____
_____
_____
_____
_____
_____
_____
_____
_____
_____
_____
_____
_____
_____
_____
_____
_____
_____
_____
_____
_____
_____
_____
_____
_____
_____
_____
_____
_____

ITALIAN SAUSAGE & EGG CROISSANTS

Wake up your taste buds with breakfast sandwiches featuring spicy sausage and fluffy egg, on a croissant.

—EMORY DOTY JASPER, GA

PREP: 25 MIN. • **COOK:** 15 MIN. • **MAKES:** 8 SERVINGS

- 1 **cup (4 ounces) crumbled blue cheese**
- 1 **jalapeno pepper, seeded and minced**
- 1 **teaspoon each dried basil, oregano and parsley flakes**
- 1 **pound bulk Italian sausage**
- 8 **eggs**
- 3 **tablespoons 2% milk**
- ⅛ **teaspoon salt**
- ⅛ **teaspoon pepper**
- 3 **tablespoons butter**
- ½ **cup mayonnaise**
- 8 **croissants, split**
- 8 **slices tomato**
- 1 **medium ripe avocado, peeled and sliced**

1. In a large bowl, combine the cheese, jalapeno and herbs. Crumble sausage over mixture and mix well. Shape into eight patties.

2. In a large nonstick skillet over medium heat, cook patties 4-5 minutes on each side or until no longer pink. Set aside and keep warm.

3. Whisk the eggs, milk, salt and pepper. In another large nonstick skillet, melt half of the butter over medium-high heat. Add half of the egg mixture to the skillet (mixture should set immediately at edges).

4. As eggs set, push cooked edges toward center, letting uncooked portion flow underneath. Cover and cook 1-2 minutes longer or until top is set. Slide eggs onto a plate; cut into four wedges. Repeat with remaining butter and egg mixture.

5. Spread mayonnaise over croissants; layer with sausage patties, eggs, tomato and avocado. Replace tops.

NOTE _Wear disposable gloves when cutting hot peppers; the oils can burn skin. Avoid touching your face._

Bacon Vegetable
Quiche

BACON VEGETABLE QUICHE

PREP: 25 MIN. • **BAKE:** 30 MIN.
MAKES: 6 SERVINGS

- 1 **unbaked pastry shell (9 inches)**
- 1 **cup sliced fresh mushrooms**
- 1 **cup chopped fresh broccoli**
- ¾ **cup chopped sweet onion**
- 2½ **teaspoons olive oil**
- 2 **cups fresh baby spinach**
- 3 **eggs, lightly beaten**
- 1 **can (5 ounces) evaporated milk**
- 1 **tablespoon minced fresh rosemary or 1 teaspoon dried rosemary, crushed**
- ¼ **teaspoon salt**
- ¼ **teaspoon pepper**
- 1 **cup (4 ounces) shredded cheddar cheese**
- 6 **bacon strips, cooked and crumbled**
- ½ **cup crumbled tomato and basil feta cheese**

1. Preheat oven to 450°. Line an unpricked pastry shell with a double thickness of heavy-duty foil. Bake 8 minutes. Remove foil; bake 5 minutes longer. Reduce oven to 375°.

2. Meanwhile, in a large skillet, saute mushrooms, broccoli and onion in oil until tender. Add spinach; cook until spinach is wilted.

3. In a bowl, whisk eggs, milk, rosemary, salt and pepper. Stir in vegetables, cheddar cheese and bacon. Pour into crust. Sprinkle with feta cheese.

4. Cover edges loosely with foil. Bake 30-35 minutes or until a knife inserted near center comes out clean. Let stand 5 minutes before cutting.

FREEZE OPTION *Cover and freeze unbaked quiche. To use, remove from freezer 30 minutes before baking (do not thaw). Preheat oven to 375°. Place quiche on a baking sheet; cover edges loosely with foil. Bake as directed, increasing time as necessary for a knife inserted near center to come out clean.*

> The best part about this recipe is you can tailor it to the season and use whatever veggies and cheese you have on hand. I especially love this in spring with fresh greens and asparagus.
> —**SHANNON KOENE** BLACKSBURG, VA

BRUNCH NOTES

GRUYERE & PROSCIUTTO STRATA

Prosciutto, sweet onions and Gruyere combine for a perfect make-ahead brunch dish, and there are never any leftovers.

—PATTI LAVELL ISLAMORADA, FL

PREP: 15 MIN. + CHILLING • **BAKE:** 35 MIN.
MAKES: 9 SERVINGS

- 2 **teaspoons canola oil**
- 4 **ounces thin slices prosciutto, chopped**
- 2 **large sweet onions, chopped (4 cups)**
- 1 **carton (8 ounces) egg substitute**
- 2½ **cups 2% milk**
- ¼ **teaspoon ground mustard**
- ⅛ **teaspoon pepper**
- 8 **cups cubed French bread**
- 1½ **cups (6 ounces) shredded Gruyere or Swiss cheese, divided**

1. In a large skillet, heat oil over medium-high heat. Add prosciutto; cook and stir until crisp. Remove from pan with a slotted spoon. Add onions to the same pan; cook and stir until tender.

2. In a bowl, whisk egg substitute, milk, mustard and pepper. Stir in bread and onions. Reserve 2 tablespoons cooked prosciutto for topping; stir remaining prosciutto into bread mixture. Transfer half of the mixture to a greased 13x9-in. baking dish; sprinkle with half of the cheese. Top with remaining bread mixture. Separately cover and refrigerate strata, reserved prosciutto and remaining cheese overnight.

3. Preheat oven to 350°. Remove strata from refrigerator while oven preheats. Bake, uncovered, 20 minutes. Top with remaining cheese, then with reserved prosciutto. Bake 15-20 minutes or until a knife inserted near center comes out clean. Let stand 5-10 minutes.

SAVORY OMELET CUPS

I replaced the pastry portion of this recipe with a light crepelike cup. Baked in tiny ovenproof dishes, they're filled with leeks, scallions, olives and sun-dried tomatoes.

—JOAN CHURCHILL DOVER, NH

PREP: 40 MIN. • **BAKE:** 10 MIN.
MAKES: 4 SERVINGS

- ¼ **cup sun-dried tomatoes (not packed in oil)**
- ½ **cup water, divided**
- 3 **eggs**
- 6 **egg whites**
- 2 **tablespoons minced fresh cilantro**
- 4 **teaspoons butter, melted**
- ½ **teaspoon salt**
- ¼ **teaspoon pepper**
- ⅓ **cup shredded provolone cheese**
- 1 **cup chopped leeks (white portion only)**
- 2 **green onions, chopped**
- 1 **tablespoon olive oil**
- 2 **tablespoons chopped Greek olives**
- 2 **teaspoons minced fresh oregano or ½ teaspoon dried oregano**
- ¼ **cup grated Parmesan cheese**
- 1 **tablespoon honey**

1. Place tomatoes in a small bowl. Cover with ¼ cup water; let stand 30 minutes.

2. Meanwhile, in a large bowl, whisk eggs, egg whites, cilantro, butter, salt, pepper and remaining water.

3. Heat an 8-in. nonstick skillet coated with cooking spray; pour about ½ cup egg mixture into center of skillet. Lift and tilt pan to evenly coat bottom. Cook 1½ to 2 minutes or until top appears dry; turn and cook 30-45 seconds longer or until set.

4. Remove from pan and press into a 1-cup baking dish or ramekin coated with cooking spray. Repeat with remaining egg mixture, making three more omelet cups (coat skillet with cooking spray as needed). Sprinkle provolone cheese into cups.

5. Preheat oven to 350°. Drain the tomatoes; chop and set aside. In a large nonstick skillet, saute leeks and onions in oil until tender. Stir in the tomatoes, olives and oregano; cook over medium heat 2-3 minutes. Spoon into omelet cups. Sprinkle with Parmesan cheese; drizzle with honey.

6. Bake the cups 10-12 minutes or until heated through.

WASHING LEEKS

Leeks have sand and dirt between the layers. To clean, cut off the dark green portion. Cut the white portion in half lengthwise. Rinse under cold running water, separating the layers to remove any grit.

BRUNCH NOTES

_____
_____
_____
_____
_____
_____
_____
_____
_____
_____
_____
_____
_____
_____
_____
_____
_____
_____
_____
_____
_____
_____
_____
_____
_____
_____
_____
_____
_____
_____
_____
_____
_____
_____
_____
_____

BRUNCH PUFFS MAIN DISH

This recipe wasn't handed down from my mother—it was passed "up" from my granddaughter! It's now a favorite dish at my home for Mother's Day and at celebrations throughout the year.
—**JUDY GOCHENOUR** LOGAN, IA

PREP: 20 MIN. • **BAKE:** 35 MIN. + COOLING
MAKES: 8 SERVINGS

- 1 **cup water**
- ½ **cup butter**
- ½ **teaspoon salt**
- 1 **cup all-purpose flour**
- 4 **eggs**

FILLING
- ½ **cup chopped green pepper**
- ½ **cup chopped onion**
- 1 **tablespoon butter**
- 8 **eggs**
- ½ **teaspoon salt**
- ¼ **teaspoon pepper**
- 1 **cup chopped fully cooked ham**
- 1 **cup (4 ounces) shredded cheddar cheese**

1. Preheat oven to 400°. In a large saucepan, bring water, butter and salt to a boil. Add flour all at once and stir until a smooth ball forms. Remove from heat; let stand 5 minutes. Add eggs, one at a time, beating well after each addition. Beat until mixture is smooth and shiny.

2. Drop by ¼ cupfuls 2 in. apart onto a greased baking sheet. Bake 35 minutes or until golden brown. Transfer to a wire rack. Immediately split puffs open; remove and discard tops and soft dough from inside. Set aside.

3. In a large skillet, saute green pepper and onion in butter until tender. In a medium bowl, beat eggs, salt and pepper. Add to skillet, stirring over medium heat until almost done. Add ham and cheese; stir until eggs are set. Spoon into puffs. Serve immediately.

Brunch Puffs
Main Dish

True Belgian
Waffles

Pour on
the Syrup

TRUE BELGIAN WAFFLES

START TO FINISH: 20 MIN
MAKES: 10 WAFFLES (ABOUT 4½ INCHES)

2 **cups all-purpose flour**
¾ **cup sugar**
3½ **teaspoons baking powder**
2 **eggs, separated**
1½ **cups milk**
1 **cup butter, melted**
1 **teaspoon vanilla extract**
   Sliced fresh strawberries or syrup

1. In a bowl, combine flour, sugar and baking powder. In another bowl, lightly beat egg yolks. Add the milk, butter and vanilla; mix well. Stir into the dry ingredients just until combined. Beat egg whites until stiff peaks form; fold into batter.

2. Bake in a preheated waffle iron according to manufacturer's directions until golden brown. Serve with the strawberries or syrup.

I was given this recipe while visiting my husband's relatives in Belgium. Back in the U.S., I served the waffles to his Belgian-born grandmother. She said they tasted just like home.
—**ROSE DELEMEESTER** ST. CHARLES, MI

FRENCH TOAST WITH APPLE TOPPING

You can't top this dish for breakfast or brunch. Warm apples and a hint of cinnamon make it a unique French toast.

—**JANIS SCHARNOTT** FONTANA, WI

START TO FINISH: 20 MIN.
MAKES: 2 SERVINGS

1 **medium apple, peeled and thinly sliced**
1 **tablespoon brown sugar**
¼ **teaspoon ground cinnamon**
2 **tablespoons butter, divided**
1 **egg**
¼ **cup 2% milk**
1 **teaspoon vanilla extract**
4 **slices French bread (½ inch thick)**
   Maple syrup, optional

1. In a large skillet, saute apple, brown sugar and cinnamon in 1 tablespoon butter until apple is tender.

2. In a shallow bowl, whisk the egg, milk and vanilla. Dip both sides of each bread slice in egg mixture.

3. In a skillet, melt remaining butter over medium heat. Cook bread on both sides until golden brown. Serve with apples and, if desired, maple syrup.

HAM & ASPARAGUS PUFF PANCAKE

Turn any morning into a special occasion by serving this fluffy and flavorful puff pancake. It's filled with ham and tender asparagus.

—TASTE OF HOME COOKING SCHOOL

START TO FINISH: 30 MIN.
MAKES: 6-8 SERVINGS

- ¼ **cup butter, cubed**
- 1 **cup all-purpose flour**
- 4 **eggs**
- 1 **cup milk**
- ¼ **teaspoon salt**
- ⅛ **teaspoon white pepper**

FILLING

- 3 **tablespoons butter**
- ¾ **pound (1½ cups) chopped fully cooked ham**
- ½ **pound fresh asparagus spears, trimmed and cut into 1-inch pieces**
- 2 **tablespoons all-purpose flour**
- ¾ **cup milk**
- ¼ **cup sour cream**
- 1 **teaspoon lemon juice**
- ¼ **teaspoon hot pepper sauce**
- ½ **cup shredded cheddar cheese**

1. Preheat oven to 425°. Place the butter in a 10-in. ovenproof skillet; place in oven 3-4 minutes or until melted. In a bowl, beat flour, eggs, milk, salt and pepper until smooth. Pour the mixture into prepared skillet. Bake 22-25 minutes or until puffed and golden brown.

2. Meanwhile, in a saucepan, melt butter. Add ham and asparagus; cook over medium-high heat 5 minutes, stirring occasionally. Stir in flour until blended. Gradually stir in milk. Bring to a boil; cook and stir 3 minutes. Reduce heat; stir in sour cream, lemon juice and pepper sauce.

3. Spoon into center of puff pancake. Sprinkle with cheese. Cut into wedges; serve immediately.

CORNMEAL-WHEAT HOTCAKES

Drizzled with a touch of cinnamony honey butter, these tasty hotcakes will brighten the day for everyone at the breakfast table. We sometimes add fruit on the side.

—ELISABETH LARSEN PLEASANT GROVE, UT

PREP: 15 MIN. • **COOK:** 5 MIN./BATCH
MAKES: 12 PANCAKES
(½ CUP HONEY BUTTER)

- ¾ **cup all-purpose flour**
- ½ **cup whole wheat flour**
- ¼ **cup cornmeal**
- 2 **teaspoons sugar**
- 1 **teaspoon salt**
- 1 **teaspoon baking powder**
- ¾ **teaspoon baking soda**
- 2 **eggs**
- 1½ **cups buttermilk**
- ¼ **cup canola oil**

HONEY BUTTER

- ¼ **cup butter, softened**
- ¼ **cup honey**
- 1 **teaspoon ground cinnamon**

1. In a large bowl, combine the first seven ingredients. Combine the eggs, buttermilk and oil; add to the dry ingredients just until moistened.
2. Pour batter by ¼ cupfuls onto a greased hot griddle; turn when bubbles form on top. Cook until the second side is golden brown.
3. In a small bowl, mix butter, honey and cinnamon. Serve with pancakes.

HOMEMADE PANCAKE SYRUP

This simple maple syrup cooks up in minutes but leaves a lasting impression. It's best served hot over waffles or pancakes with lots of creamy butter.

—JILL HANNS KLAMATH FALLS, OR

PREP: 15 MIN. + COOLING
MAKES: ABOUT 1½ CUPS

- ¾ **cup packed brown sugar**
- ¼ **cup sugar**
- ¾ **cup water**
- ½ **cup light corn syrup**
- ½ **teaspoon maple flavoring**
- ½ **teaspoon vanilla extract**

In a saucepan, combine the sugars, water and corn syrup; bring to a boil over medium heat. Boil 7 minutes or until slightly thickened. Remove from heat; stir in maple flavoring and vanilla. Cool 15 minutes. Serve over pancakes, waffles or French toast.

BRUNCH NOTES

_____   _____
_____   _____
_____   _____
_____   _____
_____   _____
_____   _____

TIRAMISU CREPES

Delicate crepes, filled with creamy mascarpone cheese and laced with vanilla and a hint of coffee liqueur, make for a mouthwatering morning treat. They're special in every way.

—**KAREN SHELTON** COLLIERVILLE, TN

PREP: 30 MIN. + CHILLING
COOK: 5 MIN./BATCH • **MAKES:** 22 CREPES

- 4 **eggs**
- ¾ **cup 2% milk**
- ¼ **cup club soda**
- 3 **tablespoons butter, melted**
- 2 **tablespoons strong brewed coffee**
- 1 **teaspoon vanilla extract**
- 1 **cup all-purpose flour**
- 3 **tablespoons sugar**
- 2 **tablespoons baking cocoa**
- ¼ **teaspoon salt**

FILLING

- 1 **carton (8 ounces) mascarpone cheese**
- 1 **package (8 ounces) cream cheese, softened**
- 1 **cup sugar**
- ¼ **cup coffee liqueur or strong brewed coffee**
- 2 **tablespoons vanilla extract**
  Optional toppings: chocolate syrup, whipped cream and baking cocoa

1. In a large bowl, beat the eggs, milk, club soda, butter, coffee and vanilla. Combine the flour, sugar, cocoa and salt; add to milk mixture and mix well. Cover and refrigerate for 1 hour.

2. Heat a lightly greased 8-in. nonstick skillet over medium heat; pour 2 tablespoons batter into center of skillet. Lift and tilt pan to coat bottom evenly. Cook until top appears dry; turn and cook 15-20 seconds longer. Remove to a wire rack. Repeat with remaining batter, greasing skillet as needed. When cool, stack crepes with waxed paper or paper towels in between.

3. For filling, in a large bowl, beat the cheeses and sugar until fluffy. Add liqueur and vanilla; beat until smooth. Spoon about 2 tablespoons filling down the center of each crepe; roll up. Top with chocolate syrup, whipped cream and cocoa if desired.

STRAWBERRY SYRUP

This recipe is a spinoff of my dad's homemade syrup. Our son requests it with fluffy pancakes whenever he and his family come to visit.

—**NANCY DUNAWAY** SPRINGFIELD, IL

START TO FINISH: 20 MIN.
MAKES: ABOUT 2½ CUPS

- 1 **cup sugar**
- 1 **cup water**
- 1½ **cups mashed unsweetened strawberries**

In a saucepan, bring sugar and water to a boil. Gradually add strawberries; return to a boil. Reduce heat; simmer, uncovered, 10 minutes, stirring occasionally. Serve over pancakes, waffles or ice cream.

CHOCOLATE PECAN WAFFLES

This is a yummy dish to serve for company, and it tastes equally good whether you serve it with raspberries, strawberries or bananas. The crisp and chocolaty waffles will have everyone wanting more!

—LUCILLE MEAD ILION, NY

START TO FINISH: 30 MIN.
MAKES: 16 WAFFLES

- 3 **eggs**
- 1 **cup sugar**
- 1 **cup whole milk**
- ½ **cup butter, melted**
- ¼ **teaspoon vanilla extract**
- 2 **ounces unsweetened chocolate, melted and cooled**
- 1½ **cups all-purpose flour**
- 1 **teaspoon baking powder**
- ½ **teaspoon salt**
- ¼ **teaspoon baking soda**
- ¼ **cup chopped pecans**
  Whipped topping and fresh raspberries

1. In a large bowl, beat eggs and sugar until foamy; beat in the milk, butter and vanilla. Stir in chocolate.

2. In another bowl, combine the flour, baking powder, salt and baking soda. Stir in chocolate mixture just until moistened. Fold in pecans.

3. Bake in a preheated waffle iron according to manufacturer's directions until golden brown. Serve with whipped topping and raspberries.

FREEZE OPTION *Cool waffles on wire racks. Freeze between layers of waxed paper in a resealable plastic freezer bag. To use, reheat waffles in a toaster on medium setting. Or, microwave each waffle on high for 30-60 seconds or until heated through.*

BANANAS FOSTER BAKED FRENCH TOAST

Bananas Foster for breakfast! This baked French toast serves up all the taste of the spectacular dessert in fine fashion.

—**L.G. NASSON** QUINCY, MA

PREP: 20 MIN. + CHILLING • **BAKE:** 35 MIN.
MAKES: 6 SERVINGS

- ½ **cup butter, cubed**
- ⅔ **cup packed brown sugar**
- ½ **cup heavy whipping cream**
- ½ **teaspoon ground cinnamon**
- ½ **teaspoon ground allspice**
- ¼ **cup chopped pecans, optional**
- 3 **large bananas, sliced**
- 12 **slices egg bread or challah (about ¾ pound)**
- 1½ **cups 2% milk**
- 3 **eggs**
- 1 **tablespoon sugar**
- 1 **teaspoon vanilla extract**

1. Place butter in a microwave-safe bowl; microwave, covered, 30-45 seconds or until melted. Stir in brown sugar, cream, cinnamon, allspice and, if desired, pecans. Add bananas; toss gently to coat.

2. Transfer to an ungreased 13x9-in. baking dish. Arrange bread over top, trimming to fit as necessary.

3. Place remaining ingredients in a blender; cover and process just until blended. Pour over bread. Refrigerate, covered, 8 hours or overnight.

4. Preheat oven to 375°. Remove French toast from refrigerator while oven heats. Bake, uncovered, 35-40 minutes or until a knife inserted near the center comes out clean. Let stand 5-10 minutes. To serve, invert onto a plate.

WAFFLES WITH PEACH-BERRY COMPOTE

I created my compote one summer Sunday when I was looking for a more healthful alternative to butter and maple syrup to top my waffles. I was amazed at the results!

—BRANDI WATERS FAYETTEVILLE, AR

PREP: 25 MIN. • **COOK:** 5 MIN./BATCH
MAKES: 12 WAFFLES
(1½ CUPS COMPOTE)

- 1 cup chopped peeled fresh or frozen peaches
- ½ cup orange juice
- 2 tablespoons brown sugar
- ¼ teaspoon ground cinnamon
- 1 cup fresh or frozen blueberries
- ½ cup sliced fresh or frozen strawberries

BATTER

- 1¼ cups all-purpose flour
- ½ cup whole wheat flour
- 2 tablespoons flaxseed
- 1 teaspoon baking powder
- 1 teaspoon baking soda
- ½ teaspoon ground cinnamon
- 1 cup buttermilk
- ¾ cup orange juice
- 1 tablespoon canola oil
- 1 teaspoon vanilla extract

1. In a small saucepan, combine the peaches, orange juice, brown sugar and cinnamon; bring to a boil over medium heat. Add berries; cook and stir 8-10 minutes or until thickened.

2. In a large bowl, combine the flours, flaxseed, baking powder, baking soda and cinnamon. Combine buttermilk, orange juice, oil and vanilla; stir into dry ingredients just until moistened.

3. Bake in a preheated waffle iron according to manufacturer's directions until golden brown. Serve with compote.

BRUNCH NOTES

CARDAMOM SOUR CREAM WAFFLES

Sweet with just the right amount of spice, these easy waffles make it nearly impossible to skip your morning meal.

—BARB MILLER OAKDALE, MN

PREP: 15 MIN. • **COOK:** 5 MIN./BATCH
MAKES: 14 WAFFLES

- ¾ **cup all-purpose flour**
- ¾ **cup whole wheat flour**
- 1½ **teaspoons baking powder**
- 1 **teaspoon ground cardamom**
- ¾ **teaspoon baking soda**
- ½ **teaspoon ground cinnamon**
- ¼ **teaspoon salt**
- 2 **eggs**
- 1 **cup fat-free milk**
- ¾ **cup reduced-fat sour cream**
- ½ **cup packed brown sugar**
- 1 **tablespoon butter, melted**
- 1 **teaspoon vanilla extract**

1. In a large bowl, combine the first seven ingredients. In another bowl, whisk the eggs, milk, sour cream, brown sugar, butter and vanilla. Stir into dry ingredients just until combined.

2. Bake in a preheated waffle iron according to manufacturer's directions until golden brown.

Cardamom
Sour Cream Waffles

STRAWBERRY MASCARPONE CREPES

These lovely crepes were my mom's Sunday-morning specialty. She grew all her own herbs, including plenty of basil for this recipe and other favorites.

—**SHANNON SOPER** WEST BEND, WI

PREP: 45 MIN. + STANDING
COOK: 20 MIN. • **MAKES:** 8 CREPES

BATTER
- 3 **eggs**
- ¾ **cup plus 2 tablespoons milk**
- ¾ **cup all-purpose flour**
- 5 **teaspoons butter, melted**
- 1 **tablespoon sugar**
- 1 **teaspoon vanilla extract**
- ¼ **teaspoon salt**

FILLING
- 1 **cup (8 ounces) mascarpone cheese**
- 2 **tablespoons confectioners' sugar**
- 3 **to 4 teaspoons minced fresh basil**
- 1 **teaspoon lemon juice**
- 1½ **cups sliced fresh strawberries**

STRAWBERRY TOPPING
- 2 **cups sliced fresh strawberries**
- ½ **cup sugar**
- 2 **tablespoons orange juice**
- 1 **teaspoon strawberry or vanilla extract**
  Dash salt
- 4 **teaspoons butter, divided**

1. In a blender, combine the batter ingredients; cover and process until smooth. Cover and refrigerate 1 hour.

2. Meanwhile, for filling, in a bowl, combine the cheese, confectioners' sugar, basil and lemon juice. Gently fold in strawberries. Cover and refrigerate at least 30 minutes.

3. For topping, in a bowl, combine the strawberries, sugar, orange juice, extract and salt. Let stand 30 minutes.

4. Melt 1 teaspoon butter in an 8-in. nonstick skillet over medium heat; pour about ¼ cup batter into center of skillet. Lift and tilt pan to coat bottom evenly. Cook until top appears dry; turn and cook 15-20 seconds longer. Remove to a wire rack. Repeat with remaining batter, greasing skillet as needed. When cool, stack crepes with waxed paper or paper towels in between.

5. Spoon filling over crepes; roll up. Serve with strawberry topping.

BLUEBERRY SYRUP

Blueberries and blueberry preserves make this syrup burst with flavor. Try it over your favorite waffles, French toast or pancakes.

—**LORRIE MCCURDY** FARMINGTON, NM

START TO FINISH: 15 MIN.
MAKES: ABOUT 2 CUPS

- 1 **cup packed brown sugar**
- 1 **cup sugar**
- ½ **cup fresh or frozen blueberries**
- ½ **cup water**
- ½ **cup blueberry preserves**
- 1 **teaspoon maple flavoring**

In a saucepan, combine the sugars, blueberries and water. Bring to a boil; cook and stir 2 minutes. Remove from heat; stir in the preserves and maple flavoring. Refrigerate leftovers.

ORANGE RICOTTA PANCAKES

These popular pancakes are likely to spark a craving. They're so moist and tender you could even eat them without syrup!

—**BREHAN KOHL** ANCHORAGE, AK

START TO FINISH: 30 MIN.
MAKES: 12 PANCAKES

- 1½ cups all-purpose flour
- 3 tablespoons sugar
- 1½ teaspoons baking powder
- ½ teaspoon baking soda
- ¼ teaspoon salt
- 1 egg
- 1 cup part-skim ricotta cheese
- ¾ cup 2% milk
- ½ teaspoon grated orange peel
- ½ cup orange juice
- ¼ cup butter, melted
- ½ teaspoon vanilla extract
  Maple syrup and confectioners' sugar

1. In a large bowl, whisk the first five ingredients. In another bowl, whisk egg, cheese, milk, orange peel, orange juice, melted butter and vanilla until blended. Add to dry ingredients; stir just until moistened.

2. Lightly grease a griddle; heat over medium heat. Pour batter by ¼ cupfuls onto griddle. Cook until bubbles on top begin to pop and bottoms are golden brown. Turn; cook until second side is golden brown. Serve with syrup and confectioners' sugar.

CHOCOLATE-FRUIT CREPES

These pretty dessert crepes are delicate, delightful and as simple to make as they are special! They're nice for a fancy brunch, too.

—LAURA MCDOWELL LAKE VILLA, IL

PREP: 30 MIN. + CHILLING
COOK: 5 MIN./BATCH
MAKES: 10 SERVINGS

- 1½ **cups buttermilk**
- 3 **eggs**
- 3 **tablespoons butter, melted**
- 1 **cup all-purpose flour**
- 2 **tablespoons sugar**
- 2 **tablespoons baking cocoa**

FILLING

- 1 **can (21 ounces) cherry pie filling**
- 1 **can (8½ ounces) sliced peaches, drained and chopped**
- ½ **teaspoon ground cinnamon**
- ⅛ **teaspoon almond extract**
- ⅓ **cup hot fudge ice cream topping, warmed**
  Whipped cream, optional

1. In a large bowl, combine the buttermilk, eggs and butter. Combine the flour, sugar and cocoa; add to buttermilk mixture and mix well. Cover and refrigerate for 1 hour.

2. Heat a lightly greased 8-in. nonstick skillet over medium heat; pour 2 tablespoons batter into the center of skillet. Lift and tilt pan to coat bottom evenly. Cook until top appears dry; turn and cook 15-20 seconds longer. Remove to a wire rack. Repeat with remaining batter, greasing skillet as needed. When cool, stack crepes with waxed paper or paper towels in between.

3. In a microwave-safe bowl, combine the pie filling, peaches and cinnamon. Microwave, uncovered, on high 3-4 minutes or until heated through, stirring once. Stir in extract. Spoon 2 tablespoons filling down center of each crepe. Fold sides over filling. Drizzle with ice cream topping and, if desired, garnish with whipped cream.

OVERNIGHT YEAST PANCAKES WITH BLUEBERRY SYRUP

PREP: 25 MIN. + CHILLING
COOK: 5 MIN./BATCH
MAKES: 18 PANCAKES (1 CUP SYRUP)

- 1 package (¼ ounce) active dry yeast
- 1½ cups warm buttermilk (110° to 115°)
- 1 cup all-purpose flour
- 1 cup whole wheat flour
- ¼ cup sugar
- 3 teaspoons baking powder
- 1 teaspoon baking soda
- ½ teaspoon salt
- 2 eggs
- 2 tablespoons canola oil
- 1 teaspoon vanilla extract

SYRUP

- 2 tablespoons sugar
- 2 teaspoons cornstarch
- ⅛ teaspoon salt
- ½ cup water
- ¼ cup maple syrup
- 1 cup fresh or frozen unsweetened blueberries

1. In a small bowl, dissolve yeast in buttermilk; let stand 5 minutes.

2. Meanwhile, in a large bowl, combine the flours, sugar, baking powder, baking soda and salt. Whisk the eggs, oil and vanilla; stir into dry ingredients just until moistened. Stir in yeast mixture. Cover and refrigerate for 8 hours or overnight.

3. To make pancakes, pour batter by ¼ cupfuls onto a hot griddle coated with cooking spray; turn when bubbles form on top of pancakes. Cook until second side is golden brown.

4. Meanwhile, in a small saucepan, combine sugar, cornstarch and salt. Stir in water and syrup until smooth. Add blueberries. Bring to a boil. Reduce heat; simmer, uncovered, 5-7 minutes or until berries pop. Serve warm with the pancakes.

> Nothing says "good morning" like these fluffy pancakes topped with a fruity homemade syrup. When I don't have the time to make the syrup, I'll sprinkle a few blueberries over the batter when I spoon it onto the griddle.
> —**KATIE WOLLGAST** FLORISSANT, MO

Bacon
Potato Waffles

BACON POTATO WAFFLES

I like to garnish these savory waffles with sour cream and chives or a simple cheese sauce. My mother used to sprinkle them with a touch of sugar.

—LAURA FALL-SUTTON BUHL, ID

PREP: 20 MIN. • **COOK:** 5 MIN./BATCH
MAKES: 12 WAFFLES

- 1 **cup all-purpose flour**
- 2 **tablespoons sugar**
- 2 **teaspoons baking powder**
- ½ **teaspoon salt**
- 2 **eggs**
- 1½ **cups mashed potatoes (with added milk and butter)**
- 1 **cup 2% milk**
- 5 **tablespoons canola oil**
- ¼ **cup finely chopped onion**
- 3 **bacon strips, cooked and crumbled**
  Maple syrup or chunky applesauce
  Additional crumbled cooked bacon, optional

1. In a large bowl, combine the flour, sugar, baking powder and salt. In another bowl, whisk the eggs, mashed potatoes, milk and oil. Stir into dry ingredients just until moistened. Fold in onion and bacon.

2. Bake in a preheated waffle iron according to manufacturer's directions until golden brown. Serve with syrup or applesauce. Sprinkle with additional bacon if desired.

BACON AT THE READY

As long as you are cooking bacon for breakfast, you might as well cook the entire package at the same time. Leftover bacon can be used in many dishes, including salads, sandwiches and soups.

APPLE-CHEDDAR PANCAKES WITH BACON

After tasting a scrumptious grilled apple-and-cheese sandwich, I decided to try the same flavors with pancakes. My bacon-fanatic sister suggested adding—you guessed it—bacon to the mix!

—**KIM KORVER** ORANGE CITY, IA

PREP: 15 MIN. • **COOK:** 5 MIN./BATCH
MAKES: 16 PANCAKES

- 2 **eggs**
- 1 **cup 2% milk**
- 2 **cups biscuit/baking mix**
- 8 **bacon strips, cooked and crumbled**
- 2 **large apples, peeled and shredded**
- 1½ **cups (6 ounces) shredded cheddar cheese**
  Butter and maple syrup, optional

1. In a large bowl, whisk eggs and milk until blended. Add biscuit mix and bacon; stir just until moistened. Fold in apples and cheese.

2. Lightly grease a griddle; heat over medium heat. Drop batter by ¼ cupfuls onto griddle, spreading with the back of a spoon as necessary. Cook until bubbles on top begin to pop and bottoms are golden brown. Turn; cook until second side is golden brown. If desired, serve with butter and syrup.

RED VELVET WAFFLES WITH COCONUT SYRUP

This recipe is a favorite because my daughter loves red velvet cake and I'm always looking for ways to use pecans.
—CHERYL PERRY HERTFORD, NC

PREP: 25 MIN. • **BAKE:** 5 MIN./BATCH
MAKES: 7 ROUND WAFFLES
(1 CUP TOPPING AND 2 CUPS SYRUP)

- 2 **cups all-purpose flour**
- ¾ **cup sugar**
- ¼ **cup baking cocoa**
- 1 **teaspoon baking soda**
- ¼ **teaspoon salt**
- 2 **eggs**
- 2 **cups buttermilk**
- ¼ **cup butter, melted**
- 3 **tablespoons red food coloring**
- 1 **teaspoon vanilla extract**

TOPPING
- ¾ **cup butter, softened**
- 4 **ounces cream cheese, softened**
- ½ **teaspoon ground cinnamon**
- ½ **cup finely chopped pecans**

SYRUP
- 2 **cups light corn syrup**
- ½ **cup flaked coconut, toasted**
- 1 **teaspoon coconut extract**

1. In a bowl, combine the flour, sugar, cocoa, baking soda and salt. In a large bowl, whisk the eggs, buttermilk, butter, food coloring and vanilla. Stir into dry ingredients just until moistened.
2. Bake in a preheated round Belgian waffle iron according to manufacturer's directions until golden brown.
3. Meanwhile, in a small bowl, beat the butter, cream cheese and cinnamon until smooth; stir in pecans. In another bowl, combine the corn syrup, coconut and extract. Serve topping and syrup with waffles.

OATMEAL WAFFLES

These healthful, good-tasting waffles are a tried-and-true family favorite—even with our two children. A hearty breakfast really gets us going.
—MARNA HEITZ FARLEY, IA

START TO FINISH: 30 MIN.
MAKES: 6 WAFFLES

- 1½ **cups all-purpose flour**
- 1 **cup quick-cooking oats**
- 3 **teaspoons baking powder**
- ½ **teaspoon ground cinnamon**
- ¼ **teaspoon salt, optional**
- 2 **eggs, lightly beaten**
- 1½ **cups milk**
- 6 **tablespoons butter, melted**
- 2 **tablespoons brown sugar**
  Assorted fresh fruit and yogurt

1. In a large bowl, combine flour, oats, baking powder, cinnamon and, if desired, salt; set aside. In a small bowl, whisk eggs, milk, butter and brown sugar. Add to flour mixture; stir until blended.
2. Bake in a preheated waffle iron according to manufacturer's directions until golden brown. Top with fresh fruit and yogurt.

Orange-Coconut
French Toast

ORANGE-COCONUT FRENCH TOAST

You'll think you woke up in the tropics when you dive into this French toast breakfast. There's a bright, citrusy flavor and a wonderful blend of textures in every slice.

—CAROL GILLESPIE CHAMBERSBURG, PA

PREP: 20 MIN. • **COOK:** 10 MIN./BATCH
MAKES: 4 SERVINGS

- 1 **can (13.66 ounces) coconut milk**
- 2 **eggs**
- ½ **cup orange juice**
- 1 **teaspoon vanilla extract**
- ½ **teaspoon orange extract**
- ½ **teaspoon salt**
- 1 **cup flaked coconut, toasted, divided**
- 8 **slices white bakery bread (¾ inch thick)**
- ½ **cup macadamia nuts, chopped and toasted**
  Maple syrup and orange slices, optional

1. In a large bowl, whisk coconut milk, eggs, orange juice, extracts and salt. Stir in ½ cup coconut. Place bread slices in a 15x10x1-in. baking pan. Pour coconut milk mixture over bread; turn to coat. Let stand 10 minutes.

2. Toast bread on a greased hot griddle over medium heat 3-4 minutes on each side or until golden brown. Transfer to a serving platter. Sprinkle with remaining coconut and the macadamia nuts; keep warm. Serve with the maple syrup and orange slices if desired.

NOTE *To toast coconut, spread in a 15x10x1-in. baking pan. Bake at 350° for 5-10 minutes or until golden brown, stirring frequently.*

SOFTEN SHREDDED COCONUT

To soften shredded coconut that's hard, soak it in milk 30 minutes. Drain it and pat it dry on paper towels before using. The leftover coconut-flavored milk can be used within 5 days in baked goods or blended with fresh fruit for a tasty beverage.

BRUNCH NOTES

_____
_____
_____
_____
_____
_____
_____
_____
_____
_____
_____
_____
_____
_____
_____
_____
_____
_____
_____
_____
_____
_____
_____
_____
_____
_____
_____
_____
_____
_____
_____
_____
_____
_____

PORTOBELLO WAFFLES WITH BALSAMIC SYRUP

For a delightful brunch surprise, serve crisp golden waffles that have portobello mushrooms and bacon in the batter. They're topped with tangy goat cheese butter and a drizzle of sweet balsamic reduction.

—DAVID BRIDGES SHREVEPORT, LA

PREP: 40 MIN. • **COOK:** 5 MIN./BATCH
MAKES: 16 WAFFLES
(1 CUP BUTTER AND ⅓ CUP SYRUP)

- 1 **cup balsamic vinegar**
- 2 **tablespoons brown sugar**
- 2 **bacon strips, chopped**
- ½ **cup butter, softened**
- ⅓ **cup crumbled goat cheese**
- ½ **pound portobello mushrooms, stems removed, cubed**
- 2 **tablespoons olive oil**
- 1¾ **cups all-purpose flour**
- 1 **teaspoon baking powder**
- ½ **teaspoon baking soda**
- ½ **teaspoon dried thyme**
- ½ **teaspoon pepper**
- ¼ **teaspoon salt**
- 2 **eggs**
- 1½ **cups plus 2 tablespoons milk**
- ½ **cup canola oil**

1. In a saucepan, bring vinegar and brown sugar to a boil; cook until liquid is reduced to ⅓ cup. In a skillet, cook bacon until crisp. Transfer bacon and drippings to a bowl; cool slightly. Add butter and goat cheese; beat until blended.
2. In a skillet, saute mushrooms in oil until tender; cool slightly. Place ¼ cup mushrooms in a food processor. Cover and process until very finely chopped. In a bowl, mix dry ingredients. In another bowl, whisk the eggs, milk, oil and chopped mushrooms; add to dry ingredients just until moistened. Fold in the cubed mushrooms.
3. Bake in a preheated waffle iron according to manufacturer's directions until golden brown. Serve with goat cheese butter and balsamic syrup.

Portobello Waffles
with Balsamic Syrup

SWEDISH PANCAKES

When we spend the night at my mother-in-law's house, our kids beg her to make these crepelike pancakes for breakfast!

—SUSAN JOHNSON LYONS, KS

START TO FINISH: 20 MIN.
MAKES: 20 PANCAKES

- 2 **cups milk**
- 4 **eggs**
- 1 **tablespoon canola oil**
- 1½ **cups all-purpose flour**
- 3 **tablespoons sugar**
- ¼ **teaspoon salt**
  Lingonberries or raspberries
  Seedless raspberry jam or fruit spread, warmed
  Whipped topping

1. In a blender, combine the first six ingredients. Cover and process until blended. Heat a lightly greased 8-in. nonstick skillet; pour ¼ cup batter into center. Lift and tilt pan to evenly coat bottom. Cook until top appears dry; turn and cook 15-20 seconds longer.

2. Repeat with remaining batter, adding oil to skillet as needed. Stack pancakes with waxed paper or paper towels in between. Reheat in the microwave if desired.

3. Fold the pancakes into quarters; serve with berries, raspberry jam and whipped topping.

PANNKAKOR

Swedish pancakes are known as *pannkakor* in Sweden. The batter is a little thinner than for crepes and trickier to turn over. Lingonberries are the traditional topping, but sometimes the pancakes are topped with ice cream.

SAUSAGE-FILLED CREPES

I first made this recipe 30 years ago, when my children were young. It's still one of their favorites and they always request it for special occasions.

—**KAREN COLLINS** WESTMINSTER, CO

PREP: 25 MIN. + CHILLING • **BAKE:** 45 MIN.
MAKES: 8 SERVINGS

- 3 **eggs**
- 1 **cup milk**
- 1 **tablespoon canola oil**
- 1 **cup all-purpose flour**

FILLING

- 1 **pound bulk pork sausage**
- ¼ **cup chopped onion**
- 1 **package (3 ounces) cream cheese, cubed**
- ½ **cup shredded cheddar cheese**
- ¼ **teaspoon dried marjoram**
- ½ **cup sour cream**
- ¼ **cup butter, softened**
  Minced fresh parsley

1. In a small bowl, combine eggs, milk and oil. Add flour and mix well. Cover and refrigerate 1 hour.
2. Heat a lightly greased 8-in. nonstick skillet; pour 3 tablespoons batter into center of skillet. Lift and tilt pan to coat bottom evenly. Cook until top appears dry; turn and cook 15-20 seconds longer. Remove to a wire rack. Repeat with remaining batter, greasing skillet as needed. When cool, stack crepes with waxed paper or paper towels in between.
3. Preheat oven to 375°. For filling, in a skillet, cook the sausage and onion over medium heat until meat is no longer pink; drain. Add cheeses and marjoram. Cook and stir until cheese is melted.
4. Spoon about 2 tablespoons of filling down the center of each crepe. Roll up and place seam side down in a greased 13x9-in. baking dish.
5. Cover; bake 40 minutes. Mix sour cream and butter; spoon over crepes. Bake, uncovered, 5 minutes or until edges are lightly browned and sauce is heated through. Sprinkle with parsley.

CHOCOLATE CHALLAH FRENCH TOAST

Here's a decadent French toast I serve from the kitchen of my family-run bed and breakfast.

—**MARIE PARKER** MILWAUKEE, WI

PREP: 15 MIN. + SOAKING • **COOK:** 10 MIN.
MAKES: 2 SERVINGS

- 4 **slices challah or egg bread (¾ inch thick)**
- ⅔ **cup sugar**
- ⅓ **cup baking cocoa**
- ¼ **teaspoon salt**
- ⅛ **teaspoon baking powder**
- 4 **eggs**
- 1 **cup 2% milk**
- 1 **teaspoon vanilla extract**
- 2 **tablespoons butter**
  Optional toppings: confectioners' sugar, fresh raspberries, sliced fresh strawberries, sliced ripe banana and maple syrup

1. Arrange bread slices in a 13x9-in. dish. In a bowl, combine sugar, cocoa, salt and baking powder. In another bowl, whisk eggs, milk and vanilla. Gradually whisk into dry ingredients until smooth. Pour over bread. Let stand 10 minutes, turning once.
2. In a large skillet, melt butter over medium heat. Cook bread for 3-4 minutes each side or until toasted. Serve with toppings of your choice.

Caramel-Pecan
French Toast Bake

CARAMEL-PECAN FRENCH TOAST BAKE

For a sensational dish for a Sunday brunch, try this French toast. You make it up the night before, so you only need to bake it and make the syrup the following day.

—BRAD SHUE HARPER, KS

PREP: 20 MIN. + CHILLING • **BAKE:** 30 MIN.
MAKES: 8 SERVINGS

- 1 **cup packed brown sugar**
- ½ **cup butter, cubed**
- 2 **tablespoons light corn syrup**
- 1 **cup chopped pecans, divided**
- 8 **slices French bread (¾ inch thick)**
- 6 **eggs**
- 1½ **cups 2% milk**
- 1½ **teaspoons ground cinnamon**
- 1 **teaspoon ground nutmeg**
- 1 **teaspoon vanilla extract**
- ¼ **teaspoon salt**

SAUCE
- ½ **cup packed brown sugar**
- ¼ **cup butter, cubed**
- 1 **tablespoon light corn syrup**

1. In a small saucepan, combine brown sugar, butter and corn syrup. Bring to a boil. Reduce heat; cook and stir 3-4 minutes or until thickened. Pour into a greased 13x9-in. baking dish. Sprinkle with ½ cup pecans; top with bread slices.

2. In a large bowl, whisk eggs, milk, cinnamon, nutmeg, vanilla and salt; pour evenly over bread. Sprinkle with remaining pecans. Cover and refrigerate 8 hours or overnight.

3. Remove from the refrigerator 30 minutes before baking. Preheat oven to 350°. Bake, uncovered, 30-35 minutes or until a knife inserted near center comes out clean.

4. Meanwhile, in a small saucepan, combine sauce ingredients. Bring to a boil. Reduce heat; cook and stir 2 minutes or until thickened. Serve with French toast.

3. In a microwave, melt the butter, honey and cinnamon; stir until smooth. Serve syrup with waffles.

HONEY WHEAT PANCAKES

Even my kids love these wholesome pancakes! These thick and tender pancakes have a delightful hint of honey and spice that you'll love.

—**MARTINA BIAS** BELLEVILLE, IL

PREP: 10 MIN. • **COOK:** 5 MIN./BATCH
MAKES: 12 PANCAKES

- 1½ **cups reduced-fat biscuit/baking mix**
- ½ **cup whole wheat flour**
- ¼ **cup wheat germ**
- 1 **teaspoon baking powder**
- 1 **teaspoon ground cinnamon**
- 2 **eggs, lightly beaten**
- 1½ **cups buttermilk**
- 1 **medium ripe banana, mashed**
- 2 **tablespoons honey**
  Assorted fresh fruit and/or maple syrup, optional

1. In a small bowl, combine the first five ingredients. Combine the eggs, buttermilk, banana and honey; add to dry ingredients just until moistened.
2. Pour batter by ¼ cupfuls onto a hot griddle coated with cooking spray; turn when bubbles form on top. Cook until the second side is golden brown. Serve with fruit and/or syrup if desired.

EASY MORNING WAFFLES

Making your own fluffy waffles from scratch takes no time at all, and the touch of cinnamon takes them beyond any store-bought frozen version.

—*TASTE OF HOME* TEST KITCHEN

PREP: 20 MIN. • **COOK:** 5 MIN./BATCH
MAKES: 14 WAFFLES (1 CUP SYRUP)

- 2 **cups all-purpose flour**
- 1 **tablespoon brown sugar**
- 2 **teaspoons baking powder**
- ½ **teaspoon salt**
- ½ **teaspoon ground cinnamon**
- 3 **eggs, separated**
- 2 **cups 2% milk**
- ¼ **cup canola oil**
- ¾ **teaspoon vanilla extract**
SYRUP
- ½ **cup butter, cubed**
- ½ **cup honey**
- 1 **teaspoon ground cinnamon**

1. In a large bowl, combine the flour, brown sugar, baking powder, salt and cinnamon. In a small bowl, whisk the egg yolks, milk, oil and vanilla; stir into dry ingredients just until moistened. In a small bowl, beat egg whites until stiff peaks form; fold into batter.
2. Bake in a preheated waffle iron according to manufacturer's directions until golden brown.

LATKES WITH LOX

Lox, a salty smoked salmon, is a year-round delicacy. This recipe, inspired by one from the *Jewish Journal*, uses lox as a topping.

—*TASTE OF HOME* TEST KITCHEN

PREP: 20 MIN. • **COOK:** 5 MIN./BATCH
MAKES: 3 DOZEN

- 2 **cups finely chopped onion**
- ¼ **cup all-purpose flour**
- 6 **garlic cloves, minced**
- 2 **teaspoons salt**
- 1 **teaspoon coarsely ground pepper**
- 4 **eggs, lightly beaten**
- 4 **pounds russet potatoes, peeled and shredded**
- ¾ **cup canola oil**

TOPPINGS
- 4 **ounces lox**
  Sour cream and minced fresh chives, optional

1. In a large bowl, combine the first five ingredients. Stir in eggs until blended. Add potatoes; toss to coat.

2. Heat 2 tablespoons oil in a large nonstick skillet over medium heat. Drop batter by ¼ cupfuls into oil; press lightly to flatten. Fry in batches until golden brown on both sides, using remaining oil as needed. Drain on paper towels. Serve with lox; top with sour cream and chives if desired.

Mascarpone-Stuffed French Toast
with Triple Berry Topping

MASCARPONE-STUFFED FRENCH TOAST WITH TRIPLE BERRY TOPPING

I love making this delicious French toast for my family. With a creamy filling of mascarpone cheese and a sauce of mixed berries, it's an easy-to-make breakfast treat that looks as if you spent all morning preparing it.

—**PAMELA SHANK** PARKERSBURG, WV

PREP: 20 MIN. • **COOK:** 10 MIN./BATCH
MAKES: 6 SERVINGS (4 CUPS SAUCE)

- ½ cup sugar
- 3 tablespoons cornstarch
- ¼ teaspoon salt
- ½ cup water
- 1 package (12 ounces) frozen unsweetened mixed berries
- 2 cups coarsely chopped fresh strawberries or blueberries
- 1 loaf (1 pound) challah or egg bread, cut into 12 slices
- 6 tablespoons mascarpone cheese
- 6 eggs
- 1½ cups heavy whipping cream
- ¾ cup 2% milk
- 3 teaspoons ground cinnamon
- ¾ teaspoon vanilla extract
- 4 tablespoons butter

1. In a saucepan, combine sugar, cornstarch and salt. Whisk in water. Stir in frozen berries. Bring to a boil; cook and stir 1-2 minutes or until thickened. Remove from heat; stir in fresh berries.

2. On each of 6 bread slices, spread 1 tablespoon mascarpone to within ½ in. of edges. Top with remaining bread. In a large shallow bowl, whisk eggs, cream, milk, cinnamon and vanilla.

3. In a large skillet, heat 2 tablespoons butter over medium heat. Dip both sides of sandwiches in the egg mixture, allowing each side to soak 2 minutes. Place three sandwiches in skillet; toast 4-5 minutes on each side or until golden brown. Repeat with remaining butter and sandwiches. Serve with warm berry sauce.

BANANA CHIP PANCAKES

START TO FINISH: 30 MIN.
MAKES: 12 PANCAKES

- 2 **cups biscuit/baking mix**
- 1 **egg**
- 1 **cup milk**
- 1 **cup mashed ripe bananas**
- ¾ **cup swirled milk chocolate and peanut butter chips**
  Maple syrup and additional swirled milk chocolate and peanut butter chips, optional

1. Place biscuit mix in a large bowl. Combine the egg, milk and bananas; stir into biscuit mix just until moistened. Stir in chips.

2. Pour batter by ¼ cupfuls onto a greased hot griddle; turn when bubbles form on top. Cook until the second side is golden brown. Serve with syrup and additional chips if desired.

Banana Chip
Pancakes

A birthday-morning special, these fluffy pancakes can be flavor-adjusted to your heart's content! One of my kids eats the plain banana pancakes, another likes just chocolate chips added, and a third one goes for the works.

—CHRISTEEN PRZEPIOSKI NEWARK, CA

SPICY HASH BROWN WAFFLES WITH FRIED EGGS

Refrigerated hash brown potatoes help you make quick work of these crunchy waffles. Put out lots of toppings so everyone can design his or her own plate.

—NANCY JUDD ALPINE, UT

START TO FINISH: 30 MIN.
MAKES: 4 SERVINGS

- 5 **eggs**
- ½ **teaspoon salt**
- ½ **teaspoon ground cumin**
- ½ **teaspoon pepper**
- ¼ **teaspoon chili powder**
- 1¾ **cups refrigerated shredded hash brown potatoes**
- 1 **small onion, finely chopped**
- ¼ **cup canned chopped green chilies**
- 2 **tablespoons salsa**
- 2 **tablespoons canola oil**
- ½ **cup shredded cheddar-Monterey Jack cheese**
  Optional toppings: salsa, guacamole, sour cream and minced fresh cilantro

1. In a bowl, whisk 1 egg, salt, cumin, pepper and chili powder. Stir in potatoes, onion, green chilies and salsa. Bake in a preheated waffle iron coated with cooking spray until golden brown and potatoes are tender, about 8-12 minutes.

2. In a large skillet, heat oil over medium-high heat. Break remaining eggs, one at a time, into the pan. Reduce the heat to low. Cook to desired doneness, turning after whites are set if desired. Remove from heat. Sprinkle with the cheese; cover and let stand 3 minutes or until melted.

3. Serve eggs with waffles and toppings of your choice.

CINNAMON APPLE SYRUP

Cinnamon and vanilla take center stage in this easy syrup. People enjoy it over both pancakes and crepes.

—ALBERTA MCKAY BARTLESVILLE, OK

START TO FINISH: 15 MIN.
MAKES: 1½ CUPS

- 2 **tablespoons cornstarch**
- ½ **teaspoon ground cinnamon**
- ⅛ **teaspoon salt**
- 1 **cup water**
- ¾ **cup thawed unsweetened apple juice concentrate**
- ½ **teaspoon vanilla extract**

1. In a small saucepan, mix cornstarch, cinnamon and salt. Gradually stir in the water and apple juice concentrate until smooth. Bring to a boil; cook and stir 2 minutes or until thickened.
2. Remove from heat; stir in vanilla. Serve warm. Refrigerate leftovers.

BLUEBERRY CHEESECAKE FLAPJACKS

This stunning stack of flapjacks is downright pretty. It's tempting to just sit and stare at them, but not for long! Pair them with your favorite breakfast meat and dig in.

—DONNA CLINE PENSACOLA, FL

PREP: 30 MIN. • **COOK:** 5 MIN./BATCH
MAKES: 12 PANCAKES (¾ CUP TOPPING)

- 1 **package (3 ounces) cream cheese, softened**
- ¾ **cup whipped topping**
- 1 **cup all-purpose flour**
- ½ **cup graham cracker crumbs**
- 1 **tablespoon sugar**
- 1 **teaspoon baking powder**
- ½ **teaspoon baking soda**
- ¼ **teaspoon salt**
- 2 **eggs, lightly beaten**

- 1¼ **cups buttermilk**
- ¼ **cup butter, melted**
- 1 **cup fresh or frozen blueberries**
- ¾ **cup maple syrup, warmed**
  Additional blueberries, optional

1. For topping, in a small bowl, beat cream cheese and whipped topping until smooth. Chill until serving.
2. In a large bowl, combine the flour, cracker crumbs, sugar, baking powder, baking soda and salt. Combine the eggs, buttermilk and butter; add to the dry ingredients just until moistened. Fold in blueberries.
3. Pour batter by ¼ cupfuls onto a greased hot griddle; turn when bubbles form on top. Cook until the second side is golden brown. Spread topping over pancakes. Top with warm maple syrup; sprinkle with additional blueberries if desired.

NOTE *If using frozen blueberries, do not thaw them before adding to the pancake batter. Be sure to thaw any berries used in the optional garnish.*

APPLE PANCAKES WITH CIDER SYRUP

What a delightful way to start the day! Sweet apple flavor fills every delectable bite of these hotcakes. For an extra-special treat, top with sour cream and then add syrup.

—JANET VARDAMAN ZEPHYRHILLS, FL

START TO FINISH: 30 MIN.
MAKES: 12 PANCAKES (1¼ CUPS SYRUP)

- 2 **cups complete pancake mix**
- 1½ **cups water**
- ¾ **cup grated apple**
- ½ **teaspoon ground cinnamon**

CIDER SYRUP
- ½ **cup sugar**
- 1 **tablespoon cornstarch**
- ⅛ **teaspoon ground cinnamon**
- ⅛ **teaspoon ground nutmeg**
- 1 **cup apple cider or juice**
- 2 **tablespoons butter, cubed**
- 1 **tablespoon lemon juice**

1. In a small bowl, stir the pancake mix, water, apple and cinnamon just until moistened.
2. Pour batter by ¼ cupfuls onto a greased hot griddle; turn when bubbles form on top. Cook until second side is golden brown.

3. Meanwhile, for syrup, in a small saucepan, combine sugar, cornstarch, cinnamon and nutmeg. Stir in cider until smooth. Cook and stir over medium-high heat until thickened and bubbly, about 5 minutes. Reduce heat to low; cook and stir 2 minutes longer. Stir in butter and lemon juice. Serve with the pancakes.

PECAN-ORANGE FRENCH TOAST

Thick bread slices, a touch of grated orange peel and crunchy pecans make this French toast something special.

—ALLAN WHYTOCK LEBANON, OR

PREP: 10 MIN. + CHILLING • **BAKE:** 20 MIN.
MAKES: 6 SERVINGS

- 4 **eggs**
- ⅔ **cup orange juice**
- ⅓ **cup 2% milk**
- ¼ **cup sugar**
- 1 **tablespoon grated orange peel**
- ½ **teaspoon vanilla extract**
- ¼ **teaspoon ground nutmeg**
- 6 **slices Italian bread (1 inch thick)**
- ⅓ **cup butter, melted**
- ¾ **cup chopped pecans**
  Maple syrup

1. In a small bowl, whisk the first seven ingredients. Place bread in a 13x9-in. dish; pour the egg mixture over the top. Cover and refrigerate overnight, turning slices once.
2. Preheat oven to 400°. Pour butter into a 15x10x1-in. baking pan; top with bread. Sprinkle with pecans. Bake 20-25 minutes or until golden brown. Serve with syrup.

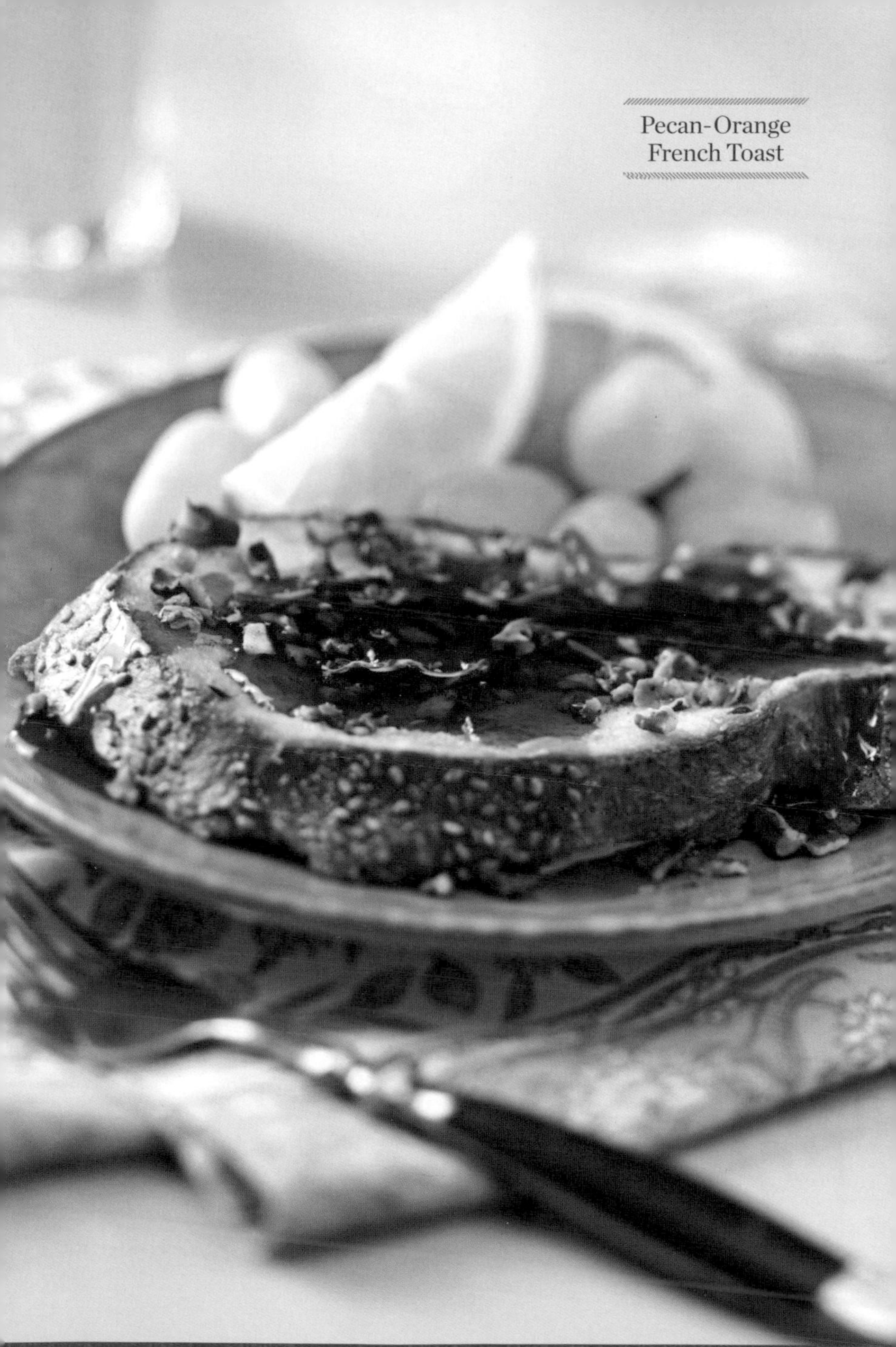

Pecan-Orange French Toast

OVERNIGHT YEAST WAFFLES

Starting the day with an appealing, hearty breakfast is certainly a step in the right direction when you're trying to follow a healthy eating plan. These waffles are so good that I even freeze them for breakfast on busy mornings.

—MARY BALCOMB FLORENCE, OR

PREP: 15 MIN. + CHILLING
COOK: 5 MIN./BATCH
MAKES: 10 SERVINGS

- 1 **package (¼ ounce) active dry yeast**
- ½ **cup warm water (110° to 115°)**
- 1 **teaspoon sugar**
- 2 **cups warm milk (110° to 115°)**
- ½ **cup butter, melted**
- 2 **eggs, lightly beaten**
- 2 **cups all-purpose flour**
- 1 **teaspoon salt**

1. In a large bowl, dissolve yeast in warm water. Add sugar; let stand for 5 minutes. Add the milk, butter and eggs; mix well. Combine flour and salt; stir into the milk mixture. Cover and refrigerate overnight.
2. Stir batter. Bake waffles in a preheated waffle iron according to manufacturer's directions until golden brown.

DIY WHIPPED BUTTER

Like the whipped butter served at restaurants? It's easy to do. Beat softened butter with an electric mixer until light and fluffy and flavor with confectioners' sugar, honey or spices.

SWEET POTATO PANCAKES WITH CARAMEL SAUCE

Sometimes sweet potatoes end up as leftovers. But by happy chance, they go well in pancake batter. Topped with caramel sauce, butter and toasted cashews, they look nothing like yesterday's forgotten dish. Don't have leftovers? Use canned sweet potatoes.

—SHERYL LITTLE SHERWOOD, AR

PREP: 25 MIN. • **COOK:** 10 MIN./BATCH
MAKES: 7 SERVINGS

- 2 **cups all-purpose flour**
- 2 **tablespoons packed brown sugar**
- 3 **teaspoons baking powder**
- ½ **teaspoon salt**
- ½ **teaspoon ground ginger**
- ¼ **teaspoon ground allspice**
- ¼ **teaspoon ground cinnamon**
- ¼ **teaspoon ground nutmeg**
- 1 **egg**
- 1¾ **cups 2% milk**
- ½ **cup canned sweet potatoes, mashed**
- 2 **tablespoons butter, melted**
- 1 **jar (12 ounces) hot caramel ice cream topping, warmed**
- ¾ **cup coarsely chopped unsalted cashews, toasted**
  Whipped butter, optional

1. In a small bowl, combine the first eight ingredients. In another bowl, whisk the egg, milk, sweet potatoes and melted butter. Stir into dry ingredients just until moistened.

2. Pour the batter by ¼ cupfuls onto a greased hot griddle; turn when bubbles form on top. Cook until the second side is golden brown.

3. Drizzle with the caramel topping; sprinkle with nuts. Serve with whipped butter if desired.

Maple-Glazed
Sausages

Bacon &
Beyond

MAPLE-GLAZED SAUSAGES

It's so easy to simmer up a sugar-and-spice syrup to cover a skillet full of breakfast sausages. They go well with eggs, French toast, pancakes—just about anything.
—TRUDIE HAGEN ROGGEN, CO

START TO FINISH: 20 MIN.
MAKES: 10 SERVINGS

- 2 packages (6.4 ounces each) frozen fully cooked breakfast sausage links
- 1 cup maple syrup
- ½ cup packed brown sugar
- 1 teaspoon ground cinnamon

In a large skillet, brown sausage links. In a small bowl, combine the syrup, brown sugar and cinnamon; pour over sausages. Bring to a boil. Reduce heat; simmer, uncovered, until sausages are glazed.

BACON BASICS

Once a package of bacon is opened, it should be used within a week. To store, place package in a resealable plastic bag and refrigerate. For longer storage, freeze bacon. Roll up individual strips of bacon, then wrap in plastic wrap and place in a resealable freezer bag. Freeze up to 1 month. To use, remove the number of strips you need and defrost in the microwave. Unroll strips and cook.

SAUSAGE BACON BITES

These tasty morsels are perfect with almost any egg dish or as finger foods that party guests can just pop into their mouths. Try them as a partner to fondue.
—PAT WAYMIRE YELLOW SPRINGS, OH

PREP: 20 MIN. + CHILLING • **BAKE:** 35 MIN.
MAKES: ABOUT 3½ DOZEN

- ¾ pound sliced bacon
- 2 packages (8 ounces each) frozen fully cooked breakfast sausage links, thawed
- ½ cup plus 2 tablespoons packed brown sugar, divided

1. Preheat oven to 350°. Cut bacon strips widthwise in half; cut sausage links in half. Wrap a piece of bacon around each piece of sausage. Place ½ cup brown sugar in a shallow bowl; roll sausages in sugar. Secure each with a toothpick. Place in a foil-lined 15x10x1-in. baking pan. Cover and refrigerate 4 hours or overnight.
2. Sprinkle with 1 tablespoon brown sugar. Bake 35-40 minutes or until bacon is crisp, turning once. Sprinkle with remaining brown sugar.

HOME-STYLE SAUSAGE GRAVY AND BISCUITS

My mother-in-law introduced me to her hamburger gravy, and I modified it slightly. We have this every weekend.

—MICHELE BAPST JACKSONVILLE, NC

START TO FINISH: 30 MIN.
MAKES: 8 SERVINGS

- 1 tube (16.3 ounces) large refrigerated flaky biscuits
- 1 pound bulk pork sausage
- 1 cup chopped sweet onion
- 2 tablespoons butter
- 1 envelope country gravy mix
- 1 tablespoon all-purpose flour
  Dash each garlic powder, Italian seasoning, onion powder and pepper
- 1½ cups 2% milk
- 1 cup reduced-sodium chicken broth

1. Bake biscuits according to package directions.
2. Meanwhile, in a skillet, cook sausage and onion over medium heat until sausage is no longer pink; drain. Add butter; cook until melted. Stir in the gravy mix, flour and seasonings until blended. Gradually add milk and broth. Bring to a boil; cook and stir 1 minute or until thickened. Serve with biscuits.

SWISS CORNED BEEF HASH

Have a St. Paddy's encore! This one-pot meal combines Irish favorites—including corned beef and potatoes—to create a satisfying dish to serve alongside eggs. Leftovers never tasted better!
—TASTE OF HOME TEST KITCHEN

PREP: 20 MIN. • **COOK:** 30 MIN.
MAKES: 4 SERVINGS

- ½ cup chopped onion
- 2 tablespoons butter
- 3 cups cubed peeled potatoes
- 1 can (14½ ounces) beef broth
- 1 cup chopped carrots
- ½ teaspoon salt
- ¼ teaspoon pepper
- 6 ounces cooked corned beef brisket, chopped (about 1½ cups)
- 2 tablespoons minced fresh parsley
- 1 cup (4 ounces) shredded Swiss cheese

1. In a large skillet, saute onion in butter until tender. Stir in the potatoes, broth, carrots, salt and pepper. Bring to a boil. Reduce heat to medium; cover and cook 20-25 minutes or until vegetables are tender and most of the liquid is absorbed.
2. Stir in corned beef and parsley; heat through. Sprinkle with cheese. Remove from heat. Cover and let stand 5 minutes or until cheese is melted.

PORK SAUSAGE PATTIES

With savory pork sausage patties, any breakfast gets a boost. These little beauties will certainly have the family coming back for seconds.

—CAROLE THOMSON KOMARNO, MB

START TO FINISH: 25 MIN.
MAKES: 6 SERVINGS

- 1 **egg, beaten**
- ⅓ **cup milk**
- ½ **cup chopped onion**
- 2 **tablespoons all-purpose flour**
- ⅛ **teaspoon salt**
  Dash pepper
- 1 **pound sage bulk pork sausage**

1. In a large bowl, combine the first six ingredients. Crumble sausage over mixture and mix well. Shape the mixture into six patties.
2. In a large skillet, cook patties over medium heat 6 minutes on each side or until meat is no longer pink, turning occasionally.

Sausage
Hash Skillet

SAUSAGE HASH SKILLET

I created this recipe by trying to work with what I had in the refrigerator. Regular or spicy sausage can be used, and red potatoes make it more colorful.
—**KARI CAVEN** COEUR D'ALENE, ID

START TO FINISH: 30 MIN. • **MAKES:** 2 SERVINGS

- ½ **pound bulk pork sausage**
- 2½ **cups cubed cooked potatoes**
- 1 **cup thinly sliced sweet onion**
- 1 **cup sliced fresh mushrooms**
- 2 **tablespoons butter**
- ¼ **teaspoon salt**
- ¼ **teaspoon pepper**

1. In a large heavy skillet over medium heat, cook the sausage until no longer pink; drain and set aside.

2. In the same skillet, cook potatoes, onion and mushrooms in butter until potatoes are lightly browned. Stir in the sausage, salt and pepper; heat through.

BAKED CANADIAN-STYLE BACON

Brown sugar, pineapple juice and ground mustard nicely season slices of Canadian bacon. You can easily double the recipe when entertaining a crowd.
—**MYRA INNES** AUBURN, KS

PREP: 10 MIN. • **BAKE:** 25 MIN.
MAKES: 6-8 SERVINGS

- 1 **pound sliced Canadian bacon**
- ¼ **cup packed brown sugar**
- ¼ **cup pineapple juice**
- ¼ **teaspoon ground mustard**

Preheat oven to 325°. Place bacon in a greased 11x7-in. baking dish. In a bowl, combine brown sugar, pineapple juice and mustard. Pour over the bacon. Cover and bake 25-30 minutes or until heated through.

BRUNCH NOTES

STEAK & MUSHROOM BREAKFAST HASH

Yes, we call this savory dish a breakfast hash, but with delectable ingredients such as mushrooms, zucchini, cheese and taters, we bet your family will love this meal at any time of the day.

—*TASTE OF HOME* TEST KITCHEN

START TO FINISH: 30 MIN.
MAKES: 4 SERVINGS

- 4 **medium potatoes, cubed**
- ½ **cup water**
- ½ **pound sliced fresh mushrooms**
- 1 **medium zucchini, quartered and sliced**
- 2 **tablespoons butter, divided**
- ⅔ **cup beef broth**
- 1 **tablespoon Dijon mustard**
- ¾ **teaspoon dried rosemary, crushed**
- 6 **ounces cooked sirloin steak, thinly sliced and cut into 1-inch pieces**
- 4 **eggs**
- ½ **cup shredded cheddar cheese**
  Coarsely ground pepper

1. Place the potatoes and water in a microwave-safe dish. Cover and microwave on high 9 minutes or until potatoes are tender.

2. Meanwhile, saute mushrooms and zucchini in 1 tablespoon butter in a large skillet until crisp-tender. Drain potatoes and add to the skillet. Stir in broth, mustard and rosemary. Bring to a boil. Reduce heat; simmer, uncovered, 3 minutes. Add steak; heat through.

3. Fry eggs in remaining butter in another skillet as desired. Serve with hash; sprinkle with cheese and pepper.

BREAKFAST BUNDLES

Getting kids to eat breakfast is a breeze when you offer them these little bundles of goodness packed with hearty ingredients. The recipe is so simple that kids of all ages can help make them.

—BERNICE WILLIAMS NORTH AURORA, IL

START TO FINISH: 30 MIN.
MAKES: 2 DOZEN

- ½ **cup butter, softened**
- 2 **tablespoons orange juice concentrate**
- 1 **egg, lightly beaten**
- 1½ **cups all-purpose flour**
- ⅔ **cup sugar**
- ½ **cup Grape-Nuts cereal**
- 1 **teaspoon baking powder**
- ½ **pound sliced bacon, cooked and crumbled**

1. Preheat oven to 350°. In a bowl, beat butter and orange juice. Add egg; mix well. Combine flour, sugar, cereal and baking powder; stir into butter mixture. Fold in bacon.

2. Drop by rounded tablespoonfuls onto ungreased baking sheets. Bake 11-13 minutes or until edges are light brown. Store in the refrigerator.

FREEZE OPTION *Freeze cooled bundles in resealable plastic freezer bags. To use, place bundles on an ungreased baking sheet in a preheated 350° oven until heated through.*

LITTLE SAUSAGE POCKETS

A satisfying breakfast doesn't get much quicker and easier. Just grab one of these cheesy sausage-stuffed rolls and you'll be on your way.

—CHERI HARRISON CAIRO, GA

PREP: 25 MIN. • **BAKE:** 15 MIN.
MAKES: 4 SERVINGS

- ¼ **pound bulk pork sausage, cooked and drained**
- ½ **cup shredded cheddar cheese**
- 2 **ounces cream cheese, softened**
- 1 **tablespoon dried parsley flakes**
- 1 **tube (8 ounces) refrigerated crescent rolls**

1. Preheat oven to 375°. In a small bowl, combine sausage, cheddar cheese, cream cheese and parsley.

2. Unroll crescent dough and separate into four rectangles; seal perforations. Transfer to a foil-lined baking sheet. Place 3 tablespoons sausage mixture in the center of each rectangle. Bring four corners of dough over filling and twist; pinch to seal.

3. Bake 14-16 minutes or until golden brown. Serve warm. Store leftovers in the refrigerator.

CABIN HASH

My family named this dish because I served it when we vacationed at our cabin on the Mississippi River. It's become such a favorite that I often make it when we're home.

—LYMAN HEIN ROCHESTER, MN

START TO FINISH: 30 MIN.
MAKES: 8-10 SERVINGS

- 12 **medium potatoes (about 4 pounds), peeled, cooked and cubed**
- 3 **cups cubed fully cooked ham (about 1 pound)**
- ½ **cup chopped onion**
- ½ **cup butter, cubed**
- 3 **cups frozen chopped broccoli, thawed**
  Salt and pepper to taste
  Sour cream, optional

In a large skillet, cook potatoes, ham and onion in butter, stirring frequently, until potatoes are lightly browned. Add the broccoli; heat through. Season with salt and pepper. If desired, serve with sour cream.

BRUNCH NOTES

SLOW COOKER GOETTA

My husband's grandfather, a German, introduced goetta to me when I first got married. I found a slow cooker recipe and changed some of the ingredients to make this the best goetta around. Now, many people request the recipe. It makes a lot of sausage, but it freezes well.

—**SHARON GEERS** WILMINGTON, OH

PREP: 45 MIN. • **COOK:** 4 HOURS
MAKES: 2 LOAVES (16 SLICES EACH)

- 6 **cups water**
- 2½ **cups steel-cut oats**
- 6 **bay leaves**
- 3 **tablespoons beef bouillon granules**
- ¾ **teaspoon salt**
- 1 **teaspoon each garlic powder, rubbed sage and pepper**
- ½ **teaspoon ground allspice**
- ½ **teaspoon crushed red pepper flakes**
- 2 **pounds bulk pork sausage**
- 2 **medium onions, chopped**

1. In a 5-qt. slow cooker, mix water, oats and seasonings. Cook, covered, on high 2 hours. Remove bay leaves.
2. In a large skillet, cook sausage and onions over medium heat 8-10 minutes or until no longer pink, breaking up sausage into crumbles. Drain, reserving 2 tablespoons drippings. Stir sausage mixture and reserved drippings into oats. Cook, covered, on low 2 hours.
3. Transfer the oat mixture to two plastic wrap-lined 9x5-in. loaf pans. Refrigerate, covered, overnight.
4. To serve, slice each loaf into 16 slices. In a large skillet, cook the goetta, in batches, over medium heat 3-4 minutes on each side or until lightly browned and heated through.

FREEZE OPTION *After shaping goetta in loaf pans, cool and freeze, covered, until firm. Transfer goetta to resealable plastic freezer bags or wrap securely in foil; return to freezer. To use, partially thaw in refrigerator overnight; slice and cook as directed.*

BREAKFAST SCRAMBLE

One weekend morning, my husband and I were hungry for breakfast without traditional sausage or bacon. I reached for the ground beef and tossed in other ingredients as I went. This was the fabulous, tasty result.

—**MARY LILL** ROCK CAVE, WV

PREP: 10 MIN. • **COOK:** 45 MIN.
MAKES: 4-6 SERVINGS

- 1 **pound ground beef**
- 1 **medium onion, chopped**
- 3 **cups diced peeled potatoes**
- ½ **cup water**
  Salt and pepper to taste
- 1 **can (14½ ounces) diced tomatoes, undrained**
- 4 **eggs, lightly beaten**
- 4 **ounces process cheese (Velveeta), sliced**

1. In a large skillet, cook beef and onion over medium heat until meat is no longer pink; drain. Add potatoes, water, salt and pepper. Cover and simmer 20 minutes or until potatoes are tender.
2. Add tomatoes; cook 5 minutes. Pour eggs over mixture. Cook and stir until eggs are completely set. Top with the cheese. Cover and cook 1 minute or until the cheese is melted.

Breakfast
Scramble

Breakfast
Skewers

BREAKFAST SKEWERS

These kabobs are fun, different and delicious, and they make a wonderful accompaniment to any egg dish.

—BOBI RAAB ST. PAUL, MN

START TO FINISH: 20 MIN.
MAKES: 5 SERVINGS

- 1 **package (7 ounces) frozen fully cooked breakfast sausage links, thawed**
- 1 **can (20 ounces) pineapple chunks, drained**
- 10 **medium fresh mushrooms**
- 2 **tablespoons butter, melted**
  Maple syrup

1. Cut sausages in half. On five metal or soaked wooden skewers, alternately thread the sausages, pineapple and mushrooms. Brush with the butter and syrup.

2. Grill, uncovered, over medium heat, turning and basting with syrup, 8 minutes or until sausages are lightly browned and fruit is heated through.

BREAKFAST SAUSAGE

Don't let calories keep you from enjoying breakfast sausage from time to time. Beyond the traditional pork sausage, you'll find lower-calorie options in turkey sausage, beef sausage, and pork and rice sausage. All can vary from mild to spicy.

SAVORY APPLE-CHICKEN SAUSAGE

These easy, healthy sausages taste great, and they make an elegant brunch dish. The recipe is also very versatile. It can be doubled or tripled for a crowd, and the sausage freezes well either cooked or raw.

—ANGELA BUCHANAN LONGMONT, CO

START TO FINISH: 25 MIN.
MAKES: 8 PATTIES

- 1   large tart apple, peeled and diced
- 2   teaspoons poultry seasoning
- 1   teaspoon salt
- ¼   teaspoon pepper
- 1   pound ground chicken

1. In a large bowl, combine the apple, poultry seasoning, salt and pepper. Crumble chicken over mixture and mix well. Shape into eight 3-in. patties.
2. In a large skillet coated with cooking spray, cook patties over medium heat 5-6 minutes on each side or until no longer pink.

CORNED BEEF HASH

START TO FINISH: 15 MIN.
MAKES: 2 SERVINGS

- 2   tablespoons canola oil
- 1   cup diced fully cooked corned beef
- 1   cup diced cooked potato
- ¼   cup chopped onion
- ¼   teaspoon salt
- ⅛   teaspoon pepper

In a small heavy skillet, heat oil over medium-high heat. Stir in all the remaining ingredients. Flatten mixture with a metal spatula. Cover and cook until bottom of potato mixture is crisp. Turn and brown the other side.

Here is a hearty meal that's perfect for two…or one hungry guy! It's great on its own or to serve at breakfast with a few eggs. You can also triple the recipe and take it to a barbecue as a substantial side dish.

—CARRIE CHAPLIN CLENDENIN, WV

SPICED BACON TWISTS

A sweet and savory rub makes this tasty bacon delicious and worth the bit of extra work. Extend the cooking time a bit if you like your bacon crispy.

—**GLENDA EVANS WITTNER** JOPLIN, MO

PREP: 10 MIN. • **BAKE:** 25 MIN.
MAKES: 5 SERVINGS

- ¼ **cup packed brown sugar**
- 1½ **teaspoons ground mustard**
- ⅛ **teaspoon ground cinnamon**
- ⅛ **teaspoon ground nutmeg**
  Dash cayenne pepper
- 10 **center-cut bacon strips**

1. Preheat oven to 350°. Combine the first five ingredients; rub over bacon on both sides. Twist bacon; place on a rack in a 15x10x1-in. baking pan.
2. Bake 25-30 minutes or until firm; bake longer if desired.

Pigs in a Pool

PIGS IN A POOL

My kids love sausage and pancakes, but making them during the week was out of the question. I bought the frozen variety on a stick but didn't like the calories, additives or price. This version of pigs in a blanket is a satisfying alternative that's much more cost-effective.
—**LISA DODD** GREENVILLE, SC

PREP: 45 MIN. • **BAKE:** 20 MIN.
MAKES: 12 SERVINGS

- 1 **pound reduced-fat bulk pork sausage**
- 2 **cups all-purpose flour**
- ¼ **cup sugar**
- 1 **tablespoon baking powder**
- 1 **teaspoon salt**
- ½ **teaspoon ground cinnamon**
- ¼ **teaspoon ground nutmeg**
- 1 **egg, lightly beaten**
- 2 **cups fat-free milk**
- 2 **tablespoons canola oil**
- 2 **tablespoons honey**
  Maple syrup, optional

1. Preheat oven to 350°. Coat mini-muffin cups with cooking spray. Shape sausage into forty-eight ¾-in. balls. Place meatballs on a rack coated with cooking spray in a shallow baking pan. Bake 15-20 minutes or until cooked through. Drain on paper towels.

2. In a large bowl, whisk flour, sugar, baking powder, salt and spices. In another bowl, whisk egg, milk, oil and honey until blended. Add to flour mixture; stir just until moistened.

3. Place a sausage ball into each mini-muffin cup; cover with batter. Bake 20-25 minutes or until lightly browned. Cool 5 minutes before removing from pans to wire racks. Serve warm, with syrup if desired.

FREEZE OPTION *Freeze the cooled muffins in resealable plastic freezer bags. To use, microwave each muffin on high for 20-30 seconds or until heated through.*

NOTE *This recipe was tested in a 1,100-watt microwave.*

Praline-Topped
Apple Bread

Sweet
Pastries

PRALINE-TOPPED APPLE BREAD

My heavenly loaf is perfect to serve to overnight guests.

—SONJA BLOW NIXA, MO

PREP: 30 MIN. • **BAKE:** 50 MIN. + COOLING
MAKES: 1 LOAF (16 SLICES)

- 2 cups all-purpose flour
- 2 teaspoons baking powder
- ½ teaspoon baking soda
- ½ teaspoon salt
- 1 cup sugar
- 1 cup (8 ounces) sour cream
- 2 eggs
- 3 teaspoons vanilla extract
- 1½ cups chopped peeled Granny Smith apples
- 1¼ cups chopped pecans, toasted, divided
- ½ cup butter, cubed
- ½ cup packed brown sugar

1. Preheat oven to 350°. In a large bowl, mix flour, baking powder, baking soda and salt. In another bowl, beat sugar, sour cream, eggs and vanilla until well blended. Stir into flour mixture just until moistened. Fold in apples and 1 cup pecans.

2. Transfer to a greased 9x5-in. loaf pan. Bake 50-55 minutes or until a toothpick inserted in center comes out clean. Cool in pan 10 minutes. Remove to a wire rack to cool completely.

3. In a saucepan, mix butter and brown sugar. Bring to a boil, stirring constantly to dissolve sugar; boil 1 minute. Spoon over bread. Sprinkle with remaining pecans; let stand until set.

NOTE *To toast nuts, spread in a dry nonstick skillet and heat over low heat until lightly browned, stirring occasionally.*

CINNAMON PEACH KUCHEN

With its flaky, buttery crust and sweet peach topping, this is one of my favorite coffee cakes—served warm or cold. It's a tried-and-true-recipe from my mother.

—RACHEL GARCIA COLORADO SPRINGS, CO

PREP: 25 MIN. • **BAKE:** 45 MIN. + COOLING
MAKES: 10 SERVINGS

- 2 cups all-purpose flour
- 2 tablespoons sugar
- ½ teaspoon salt
- ¼ teaspoon baking powder
- ½ cup cold butter, cubed
- 2 cans (15¼ ounces each) peach halves, drained and patted dry
- 1 cup packed brown sugar
- 1 teaspoon ground cinnamon
- 2 egg yolks, lightly beaten
- 1 cup heavy whipping cream

1. Preheat oven to 350°. In a bowl, combine flour, sugar, salt and baking powder; cut in butter until crumbly. Press onto the bottom and 1½ in. up the sides of a greased 9-in. springform pan.

2. Place pan on a baking sheet. Arrange peach halves, cut side up, in the crust. Combine brown sugar and cinnamon; sprinkle over peaches.

3. Bake 20 minutes. Combine egg yolks and cream; pour over peaches. Bake 25-30 minutes longer or until top is set. Cool on a wire rack. Refrigerate leftovers.

JUMBO BANANA-PECAN MUFFINS

For a brunch treat that's sure to bring out the smiles, try these flavorful muffins topped with a delightful streusel. They're wonderful served with fresh fruit.

—PAM IVBULS OMAHA, NE

PREP: 25 MIN. • **BAKE:** 20 MIN.
MAKES: 1 DOZEN

- 1½ cups all-purpose flour
- 1½ cups cake flour
- 1½ cups sugar
- 1½ teaspoons baking powder
- ¾ teaspoon baking soda
- ¾ teaspoon salt
- ½ teaspoon ground cinnamon
- 1½ cups mashed ripe bananas (2 to 3 medium)
- 1½ cups (12 ounces) sour cream
- 3 eggs
- 6 tablespoons butter, melted

STREUSEL
- ⅓ cup all-purpose flour
- ⅓ cup sugar
- 3 tablespoons brown sugar
- ¼ teaspoon ground cinnamon
- 3 tablespoons cold butter
- ½ cup chopped pecans

1. Preheat oven to 350°. In a large bowl, combine first seven ingredients. In another bowl, combine bananas, sour cream, eggs and butter. Stir into dry ingredients just until moistened.
2. Fill greased or paper-lined jumbo muffin cups two-thirds full. For the streusel, in a small bowl, combine flour, sugars and cinnamon. Cut in butter until crumbly; stir in pecans. Sprinkle over tops.
3. Bake 20-25 minutes or until a toothpick inserted near the center comes out clean. Cool 5 minutes before removing from pans to wire racks. Serve warm.

CHOCOLATE-ORANGE SCONES

Pancake mix is the key to this light and fluffy quick bread that kids will love. The scones go well with a cup of coffee or herbal tea.

—MARGARET WILSON SUN CITY, CA

START TO FINISH: 25 MIN.
MAKES: 8 SCONES

- 1½ cups complete buttermilk pancake mix
- ¾ cup heavy whipping cream
- 2 to 3 teaspoons grated orange peel
- 2 milk chocolate candy bars (1.55 ounces each), chopped

1. Preheat oven to 400°. In a small bowl, combine pancake mix, cream and orange peel. Turn onto a lightly floured surface; knead 6 times. Knead in the chopped chocolate.
2. Pat into a 9-in. circle. Cut into eight wedges. Separate wedges and place on a greased baking sheet. Bake 9-11 minutes or until lightly browned. Serve warm.

NEW ORLEANS BEIGNETS

These sweet French doughnuts are square instead of round and have no hole in the middle. They're a traditional part of breakfast in New Orleans.

—**BETH DAWSON** JACKSON, LA

PREP: 15 MIN. + CHILLING
COOK: 5 MIN./BATCH • **MAKES:** 4 DOZEN

- 1 package (¼ ounce) active dry yeast
- ¼ cup warm water (110° to 115°)
- 1 cup evaporated milk
- ½ cup canola oil
- ¼ cup sugar
- 1 egg
- 4½ cups self-rising flour
  Oil for deep-fat frying
  Confectioners' sugar

1. In a large bowl, dissolve yeast in warm water. Add milk, oil, sugar, egg and 2 cups flour. Beat until smooth. Stir in enough remaining flour to form a soft dough (dough will be sticky). Do not knead. Cover and refrigerate overnight.
2. Punch dough down. Turn onto a floured surface; roll into a 16x12-in. rectangle. Cut into 2-in. squares.
3. In an electric skillet or deep-fat fryer, heat oil to 375°. Fry squares, a few at a time, until golden brown on both sides. Drain on paper towels. Roll warm beignets in confectioners' sugar.
NOTE *As a substitute for each cup of self-rising flour, place 1½ teaspoons baking powder and ½ teaspoon salt in a measuring cup. Add all-purpose flour to measure 1 cup.*

CHERRY COFFEE CAKE

With its pretty layer of cherries and crunchy streusel topping, my coffee cake is welcome at breakfast or for dessert.

—GAIL BUSS BEVERLY HILLS, FL

PREP: 25 MIN. • **BAKE:** 35 MIN. + COOLING
MAKES: 12-16 SERVINGS

- **1 package yellow cake mix (regular size), divided**
- **1 cup all-purpose flour**
- **1 package (¼ ounce) active dry yeast**
- **⅔ cup warm water (120° to 130°)**
- **2 eggs, lightly beaten**
- **1 can (21 ounces) cherry pie filling**
- **⅓ cup butter, melted**

GLAZE
- **1 cup confectioners' sugar**
- **1 tablespoon corn syrup**
- **1 to 2 tablespoons water**

1. Preheat oven to 350°. In a large bowl, combine 1½ cups cake mix, flour, yeast and water until smooth. Stir in eggs until blended. Transfer to a greased 13x9-in. baking dish. Gently spoon pie filling over top.

2. In a bowl, mix butter and remaining cake mix; sprinkle over filling.

3. Bake 35-40 minutes or until lightly browned. Cool on a wire rack. In a small bowl, combine confectioners' sugar, corn syrup and enough water to achieve desired consistency. Drizzle over warm coffee cake.

ICED CINNAMON POTATO ROLLS

PREP: 25 MIN. + RISING • **BAKE:** 35 MIN.
MAKES: 1½ DOZEN

- ¾ **cup sugar**
- ¾ **cup hot mashed potatoes**
- 1½ **cups warm water (110° to 115°)**
- 2 **packages (¼ ounce each) active dry yeast**
- ½ **cup butter, softened**
- 2 **eggs**
- 2 **teaspoons salt**
- 6½ **cups all-purpose flour**

FILLING
- 1⅓ **cups packed brown sugar**
- 3 **tablespoons butter, softened**
- 3 **tablespoons heavy whipping cream**
- ½ **teaspoon ground cinnamon**

VANILLA ICING (FOR EACH PAN)
- 2 **cups confectioners' sugar**
- 3 **tablespoons heavy whipping cream, warmed**
- ½ **teaspoon vanilla extract**

1. In a large bowl, combine sugar and mashed potatoes. Add water and yeast; mix well. Cover and let rise in a warm place 1 hour.

2. Stir dough down; beat in butter, eggs and salt. Gradually stir in flour. Turn out onto a lightly floured surface; knead until smooth and elastic, about 6-8 minutes.

3. Divide dough in half. On a floured surface, roll each portion into a 12-in. square. In a small bowl, combine filling ingredients. Spread filling to within 1 in. of edges of each square. Roll up jelly-roll style. Cut each roll into nine slices. Arrange nine rolls into each of two greased 9-in.-square baking pans.

4. Cover and let rise in a warm place until doubled, about 1 hour.

5. Preheat oven to 350°. Bake 35-40 minutes or until golden brown. Mix icing ingredients and frost warm rolls.

FREEZE OPTION *Cover and freeze unrisen rolls. To use, thaw overnight in the refrigerator. Cover and let rise in a warm place until doubled, about 1½ hours. Preheat oven to 350°. Bake 35-40 minutes or until golden brown. Frost rolls as directed.*

Here is a scrumptious sweet roll recipe that my mother-in-law made frequently. Now I make them often. Maybe they'll be a hit with your family, too!

—JONAS SCHWARTZ BERNE, IN

CARAMEL-PECAN MONKEY BREAD

You can either cut this bread into generous slices or let people pick off the gooey pieces themselves, just like monkeys! No one can resist this caramel-coated bread.

—*TASTE OF HOME* TEST KITCHEN

PREP: 20 MIN. + CHILLING
BAKE: 30 MIN. + COOLING
MAKES: 1 LOAF (20 SERVINGS)

- 1 **package (¼ ounce) active dry yeast**
- ¼ **cup water (110° to 115°)**
- 1¼ **cups warm 2% milk (110° to 115°)**
- ⅓ **cup butter, melted**
- ¼ **cup sugar**
- 2 **eggs**
- 1 **teaspoon salt**
- 5 **cups all-purpose flour**

CARAMEL
- ⅔ **cup packed brown sugar**
- ¼ **cup butter, cubed**
- ¼ **cup heavy whipping cream**

ASSEMBLY
- ¾ **cup chopped pecans**
- 1 **cup sugar**
- 1 **teaspoon ground cinnamon**
- ½ **cup butter, melted**

1. In a large bowl, dissolve yeast in warm water. Add milk, butter, sugar, eggs, salt and 3 cups flour. Beat on medium speed 3 minutes. Stir in enough of the remaining flour to form a firm dough.

2. Turn onto a floured surface; knead until smooth and elastic, about 6-8 minutes. Place in a greased bowl, turning once to grease the top. Cover and refrigerate overnight.

3. For caramel, in a small saucepan, bring the brown sugar, butter and cream to a boil. Cook and stir 3 minutes. Pour half into a greased 10-in. fluted tube pan; sprinkle with half the pecans.

4. Punch dough down; shape into 40 balls (about 1¼ in. diameter). In a shallow bowl, combine sugar and cinnamon. Place melted butter in another bowl. Dip balls in butter, then roll in sugar mixture.

5. Place 20 balls in the tube pan; top with remaining caramel and pecans. Top with remaining balls. Cover and let rise until doubled, about 45 minutes.

6. Preheat oven to 350°. Bake 30-35 minutes or until golden brown. (Cover the pan loosely with foil if top browns too quickly.) Cool 10 minutes before inverting the bread onto a serving plate. Serve warm.

MONKEYING AROUND WITH BREAD

Monkey Bread is a colorful name for pull-apart bread. Unfortunately, no one really knows the origin for the name. This bread is also known as bubble loaf, Hungarian coffee cake and pinch-me cake.

GINGER PEAR MUFFINS

I've had this wonderful recipe in my files for years. The chunks of fresh pear make each bite of these muffins moist and delicious.
—**LORRAINE CALAND** SHUNIAH, ON

PREP: 25 MIN. • **BAKE:** 20 MIN.
MAKES: 1½ DOZEN

- ¾ **cup packed brown sugar**
- ⅓ **cup canola oil**
- 1 **egg**
- 1 **cup buttermilk**
- 2½ **cups all-purpose flour**
- 1 **teaspoon baking soda**
- 1 **teaspoon ground ginger**
- ½ **teaspoon salt**
- ½ **teaspoon ground cinnamon**
- 2 **cups chopped peeled fresh pears**

TOPPING

- ⅓ **cup packed brown sugar**
- ¼ **teaspoon ground ginger**
- 2 **teaspoons butter, melted**

1. Preheat oven to 350°. In a small bowl, beat brown sugar, oil and egg until well blended. Beat in buttermilk. In a small bowl, combine flour, baking soda, ginger, salt and cinnamon; gradually beat into buttermilk mixture until blended. Stir in pears. Fill paper-lined muffin cups two-thirds full.

2. For topping, combine brown sugar and ginger. Stir in butter until crumbly. Sprinkle over batter.

3. Bake 18-22 minutes or until a toothpick inserted near the center comes out clean. Cool 5 minutes before removing from pans to wire racks. Serve warm.

Almond
Coffee Cake

ALMOND COFFEE CAKE

I've been making this cake for gatherings or on cold winter mornings for a long time, and the platter still empties quickly. I think the cake is doubly delicious because of the cream cheese and white chip filling. One piece just leads to another!

—MARY SHIVERS ADA, OK

PREP: 35 MIN. + RISING • **BAKE:** 20 MIN. + COOLING
MAKES: 8-10 SERVINGS

- 1 **loaf (1 pound) frozen bread dough, thawed**
- 1 **package (8 ounces) cream cheese, softened**
- ¼ **cup sugar**
- 1 **egg**
- ½ **teaspoon almond extract**
- ¾ **cup white baking chips**
- 1 **tablespoon 2% milk**

GLAZE

- 1 **cup confectioners' sugar**
- ¼ **teaspoon almond extract**
- 1 **to 2 tablespoons 2% milk**
- ½ **cup slivered almonds, toasted**

1. On a lightly floured surface, roll dough into a 15x9-in. rectangle. Transfer to a lightly greased baking sheet.

2. In a small bowl, beat cream cheese and sugar until smooth. Beat in egg and extract (filling will be soft). Spread down center of rectangle; sprinkle with chips. On each long side, cut 1-in.-wide strips, about ½ in. from filling.

3. Starting at one end, fold alternating strips at an angle across filling. Seal ends. Cover and let rise in a warm place until doubled, about 1 hour.

4. Preheat oven to 350°. Brush coffee cake with milk. Bake 20-30 minutes or until golden brown. Cool on a wire rack.

5. For glaze, in a small bowl, mix confectioners' sugar and extract. Stir in enough milk to achieve desired consistency. Drizzle over coffee cake. Sprinkle with almonds.

BRUNCH NOTES

_____
_____
_____
_____
_____
_____
_____
_____
_____
_____
_____
_____
_____
_____
_____
_____
_____
_____
_____
_____
_____
_____
_____
_____
_____
_____
_____
_____
_____
_____
_____
_____
_____

BACON CINNAMON BUNS

I absolutely love bacon! I also love recipes that blend sweet and savory flavors, so I put chopped bacon in traditional cinnamon buns for a tasty combination.

—DANIELLE WILLIAMS NEWPORT, RI

PREP: 50 MIN. + RISING • **BAKE:** 20 MIN.
MAKES: 1 DOZEN

- 1 **package (¼ ounce) active dry yeast**
- 1 **cup warm whole milk**
   (110° to 115°)
- ¼ **cup sugar**
- ¼ **cup butter, softened**
- 1 **egg yolk**
- 1½ **teaspoons vanilla extract**
- ¾ **teaspoon salt**
- ½ **teaspoon ground nutmeg**
- 2¾ **to 3 cups all-purpose flour**

FILLING

- 5 **bacon strips, chopped**
- ½ **cup packed brown sugar**
- 1 **tablespoon maple syrup**
- 2 **teaspoons ground cinnamon**
- ½ **teaspoon ground nutmeg**

ICING

- 2 **cups confectioners' sugar**
- ½ **cup butter, softened**
- 2 **tablespoons whole milk**
- 1 **tablespoon maple syrup**

1. In a small bowl, dissolve yeast in warm milk. In a large bowl, combine sugar, butter, egg yolk, vanilla, salt, nutmeg, yeast mixture and 1 cup flour; beat on medium speed 2 minutes. Stir in enough remaining flour to form a soft dough (dough will be sticky).

2. Turn onto a floured surface; knead until smooth and elastic, about 6-8 minutes. Place in a greased bowl, turning once to grease the top. Cover with plastic wrap and let rise in a warm place until doubled, about 1 hour.

3. In a small skillet, cook bacon over medium heat until crisp. Remove with a slotted spoon; drain bacon on paper towels. Discard the drippings, reserving 2 tablespoons.

4. Wipe skillet clean if necessary. Combine the brown sugar, syrup, cinnamon, nutmeg and reserved bacon drippings in skillet; cook and stir over medium heat until blended. Cool to room temperature.

5. Punch dough down. Roll into an 18x12-in. rectangle. Spread the bacon mixture to within ½ in. of edges. Roll up jelly-roll style, starting with a short side; pinch the seams to seal. Cut into 12 rolls.

6. Place the rolls, cut side down, in a greased 13x9-in. baking dish. Cover and let rise in a warm place until doubled, about 45 minutes. Meanwhile, preheat oven to 400°. Bake 18-20 minutes or until golden brown.

7. In a small bowl, beat the icing ingredients until smooth. Spread over warm rolls. Serve warm.

OLD-FASHIONED DOUGHNUTS WITH BLACK & WHITE FROSTINGS

These finger-licking-good delicacies are so light and luscious, my family has always called them "angel food doughnuts"!

—DARLENE BRENDEN SALEM, OR

PREP: 35 MIN. + CHILLING
COOK: 5 MIN./BATCH
MAKES: ABOUT 1½ DOZEN DOUGHNUTS PLUS DOUGHNUT HOLES

- ½ cup sour cream
- ½ cup buttermilk
- 1 cup sugar
- 3 eggs
- 1 teaspoon vanilla extract
- 4 cups all-purpose flour
- 2 teaspoons baking powder
- ½ teaspoon baking soda
- ¼ teaspoon salt

Oil for deep-fat frying

FROSTING
- 2 cups confectioners' sugar
  Pinch salt
- 3 to 4 tablespoons boiling water
- 3 tablespoons butter, melted
- ½ teaspoon vanilla extract
- 2 tablespoons baking cocoa

1. In a large bowl, beat sour cream and buttermilk until smooth. Beat in sugar until smooth. Beat in eggs and vanilla just until combined. Combine flour, baking powder, baking soda and salt. Gradually add the flour mixture to buttermilk mixture just until combined (dough will be sticky). Cover and refrigerate 2-3 hours.

2. Turn dough onto a well-floured surface; knead 2-3 minutes or until smooth. Roll out to ½-in. thickness. Cut the dough with a floured 2½-in. doughnut cutter.

3. In an electric skillet or deep-fat fryer, heat oil to 375°. Fry doughnuts, a few at a time, 1 to 1½ minutes on each side or until golden brown. Fry the doughnut holes until golden brown. Drain on paper towels.

4. For frosting, combine confectioners' sugar and salt in a bowl. Stir in 3-4 tablespoons water, butter and vanilla until the desired consistency is reached. Pour half into a small bowl. Stir cocoa into remaining frosting until smooth. Dip the tops of the warm doughnuts in chocolate or vanilla frosting.

BRUNCH NOTES

ALMOND COCONUT KRINGLES

My mom was well-known for her delicious kringle. Try this tender, flaky pastry with its almond and coconut filling, and you'll be as hooked on it as we are!

—DEBORAH RICHMOND
TRABUCO CANYON, CA

PREP: 1 HOUR + CHILLING
BAKE: 25 MIN. + COOLING
MAKES: 4 KRINGLES (9 SLICES EACH)

- 2 **cups all-purpose flour**
- 1 **cup cold butter, cubed**
- 1 **cup (8 ounces) sour cream**

FILLING
- 1¼ **cups butter, softened**
- 1 **cup packed brown sugar**
- 3 **cups sliced almonds, toasted**
- 1½ **cups flaked coconut, toasted**

GLAZE
- 1 **cup confectioners' sugar**
- 1 **tablespoon butter, softened**
- 1 **teaspoon vanilla extract**
- 4 **to 6 teaspoons 2% milk**

1. Place flour in a bowl; cut in butter until crumbly. Stir in sour cream. Wrap in plastic wrap. Refrigerate overnight.
2. Preheat oven to 375°. In a bowl, cream butter and brown sugar until light and fluffy. Stir in almonds and coconut.
3. Divide dough into four portions. On a lightly floured surface, roll one portion of dough into a 12x10-in. rectangle. (Keep remaining dough refrigerated until ready to use.) Spread 1 cup filling lengthwise down the center. Fold in sides of pastry to meet in the center; pinch seam to seal. Repeat with the remaining dough and filling. Transfer to two ungreased baking sheets. Bake 23-27 minutes or until lightly browned. Remove to wire racks to cool completely.
4. Meanwhile, combine confectioners' sugar, butter, vanilla and enough milk to achieve desired consistency; drizzle over pastries.

CREAM CHEESE COILS

PREP: 30 MIN. + CHILLING • **BAKE:** 10 MIN.
MAKES: 1½ DOZEN

- 3¾ to 4¼ cups all-purpose flour
- ¾ cup sugar, divided
- 2 packages (¼ ounce each) active dry yeast
- 1½ teaspoons salt
- ¾ cup 2% milk
- ½ cup water
- ½ cup butter, cubed
- 1 egg
- 1 package (8 ounces) cream cheese, softened
- 1 egg yolk
- ½ teaspoon vanilla extract

GLAZE

- 1 cup confectioners' sugar
- ½ teaspoon vanilla extract
- 3 to 4 teaspoons water

1. In a large bowl, combine 1 cup flour, ½ cup sugar, yeast and salt. In a small saucepan, heat milk, water and butter to 120°-130°. Add to dry ingredients; beat on medium speed 2 minutes. Add the egg and ½ cup flour; beat on high 2 minutes. Stir in enough remaining flour to form a stiff dough. Cover and refrigerate 2 hours.

2. Turn dough onto a lightly floured surface; divide into 18 pieces. Shape each piece into a ball; roll each into a 15-in. rope. Holding one end of rope, loosely wrap dough around, forming a coil. Tuck end under; pinch to seal.

3. Place coils 2 in. apart on greased baking sheets. Cover and let rise until doubled, about 1 hour.

4. Preheat oven to 400°. In a small bowl, beat cream cheese, egg yolk, vanilla and remaining sugar until smooth. Using the back of a spoon, make a 1-in.-wide indentation in the center of each coil; spoon a rounded tablespoon of cream cheese mixture into each indentation.

5. Bake 10-12 minutes or until lightly browned. Remove from pans to wire racks to cool.

6. In a small bowl, mix confectioners' sugar, vanilla and enough water to achieve drizzling consistency. Drizzle the glaze over the cooled rolls. Store in the refrigerator.

These are my absolute favorite sweet rolls. They are easy to make but look as if you spent a lot of time on them. —SUSAN PECK REPUBLIC, MO

BEAR CLAWS

You don't have to head to gourmet bakeries to indulge in this sweet pastry. Our recipe lets you master rich, flaky pastries at home.

—TASTE OF HOME TEST KITCHEN

PREP: 1 HOUR + RISING • **BAKE:** 10 MIN.
MAKES: 9 ROLLS

- 1 package (¼ ounce) active dry yeast
- ½ cup warm 2% milk (110° to 115°)
- 2 tablespoons sugar
- ¾ teaspoon salt
- 1 egg, lightly beaten
- 1½ cups plus 2 tablespoons all-purpose flour

BUTTER MIXTURE

- 2 tablespoons all-purpose flour, divided
- ¾ cup cold butter, cut into tablespoon-size pieces

FILLING

- 6 tablespoons prepared almond filling or filling of your choice
- 1 egg, lightly beaten

GLAZE

- ¾ cup confectioners' sugar
- 2 to 3 teaspoons water

1. In a large bowl, dissolve yeast in warm milk. Stir in sugar, salt and egg; mix well. Add the flour all at once, stirring until mixed. Set aside.

2. For butter mixture, sprinkle 1 tablespoon flour on a work surface; place butter on surface and sprinkle with 1 teaspoon flour. Press and roll out with a rolling pin. Scrape butter from rolling pin and continue to work the butter until it forms a smooth mass without any hard lumps. Knead in remaining flour, working quickly to keep butter cold.

3. Place butter mixture on a sheet of plastic wrap and shape into a small rectangle. Cover with another sheet of plastic wrap; roll the butter mixture into a 9x6-in. rectangle. Set aside.

4. Turn dough onto a floured work surface; roll into a 14x10-in. rectangle, with a 10-in. side toward the bottom. Unwrap butter mixture; place on dough 1 in. above bottom edge and ½ in. from each side edge. Fold top half of dough over butter and pinch edges to seal.

5. Turn dough a quarter turn to the right; sprinkle lightly with additional flour. Lightly roll dough into a 16x8-in. rectangle. Fold the bottom third of rectangle up and top third down, as when folding a business letter, making a 5½x8-in. rectangle (this is called one turn). Rotate dough a quarter turn to the right. Lightly roll into a 16x8-in. rectangle and again fold into thirds, finishing second turn. Repeat rotating, rolling and folding two more times for a total of four times. Wrap loosely in plastic wrap; refrigerate 30 minutes.

6. Roll dough into a 12-in. square; cut square into three 12x4-in. strips. Spread 2 tablespoons filling down the center of each strip to within 1 in. of long edge. Fold lengthwise over filling and pinch seam to seal. Cut each strip into three pieces. With scissors, cut each piece four times from pinched seam to about ½ in. from folded side. Place 2 in. apart on greased baking sheets. Curve folded side slightly to separate strips and allow the filling to show. Cover and let rise in a warm place until almost doubled, about 1 hour.

7. Preheat oven to 400°. Brush bear claws with egg. Bake 10-14 minutes or until puffy and golden brown. Remove from the pans to wire racks. Combine glaze ingredients; brush over the warm rolls. Cool.

CINNAMON SWIRL QUICK BREAD

While cinnamon bread is a natural for breakfast, we love it so much that we enjoy it all day long. This is a nice twist on traditional cinnamon swirl yeast breads.

—HELEN RICHARDSON SHELBYVILLE, MI

PREP: 15 MIN. • **BAKE:** 45 MIN. + COOLING
MAKES: 1 LOAF

- 2 cups all-purpose flour
- 1½ cups sugar, divided
- 1 teaspoon baking soda
- ½ teaspoon salt
- 1 cup buttermilk
- 1 egg
- ¼ cup canola oil
- 3 teaspoons ground cinnamon

GLAZE
- ¼ cup confectioners' sugar
- 1½ to 2 teaspoons milk

1. Preheat oven to 350°. In a large bowl, combine flour, 1 cup sugar, baking soda and salt. Combine the buttermilk, egg and oil; stir into dry ingredients just until moistened. In a small bowl, mix cinnamon and remaining sugar.

2. Grease the bottom only of a 9x5-in. loaf pan. Pour half of the batter into pan; sprinkle with half the cinnamon-sugar. Carefully spread with remaining batter and sprinkle with remaining cinnamon-sugar; cut through batter with a knife to swirl.

3. Bake 45-50 minutes or until a toothpick inserted in center comes out clean. Cool 10 minutes; remove from pan to a wire rack to cool completely. Combine the confectioners' sugar and enough milk to reach the desired consistency; drizzle over loaf.

BUTTER NUT TWISTS

I am so excited that this special treat from my mother, Daisy, lives on in the kitchens of others. After this recipe was first published in *Taste of Home*, my mother would always smile when I told her about the calls coming in from other women around the country telling me how much they loved the recipe.

—JOYCE HALLISEY MOUNT GILEAD, NC

PREP: 30 MIN. + CHILLING • **BAKE:** 15 MIN.
MAKES: 6 DOZEN

- 2 **packages (¼ ounce each) active dry yeast**
- ¼ **cup warm water (110° to 115°)**
- 4 **cups all-purpose flour**
- ⅓ **cup sugar**
- ½ **teaspoon salt**
- 1 **cup cold butter, cubed**
- ¾ **cup buttermilk**
- 2 **eggs, lightly beaten**

FILLING

- 2 **cups ground walnuts (8 ounces)**
- 1 **cup flaked coconut**
- ⅓ **cup sugar**
- 4½ **teaspoons butter, melted**

1. In a bowl, dissolve yeast in warm water. In a bowl, mix flour, sugar and salt. Cut in butter until crumbly. Add buttermilk, eggs and yeast mixture; stir to form a soft dough. Cover with plastic wrap; refrigerate overnight.
2. Preheat oven to 350°. In another bowl, mix filling ingredients. Punch down dough; divide into three portions. On a sugared surface, roll one portion into a 12x9-in. rectangle. Sprinkle ⅓ cup filling lengthwise down one half of the dough. Fold dough in half over filling, forming a 12x4½-in. rectangle; pat down to press filling into dough. Seal edges.

3. Sprinkle an additional ⅓ cup filling down one half of the folded dough. Fold in half again, forming a 12x2¼-in. rectangle. Press to form a 12x4-in. rectangle. Cut into twenty-four ½-in. slices. Repeat with remaining dough and additional filling. Twist each slice one time and roll in remaining filling; place 2 in. apart on greased baking sheets.
4. Bake 15-18 minutes or until golden brown. Remove from pans to wire racks; serve warm or at room temperature.

LEMON POPPY SEED BREAD

If the days when you have time for baking are few and far between, try this extra-quick bread. You'll be amazed at the ease of preparation and the delicious flavor.

—KAREN DOUGHERTY FREEPORT, IL

PREP: 10 MIN. • **BAKE:** 35 MIN. + COOLING
MAKES: 2 LOAVES (16 SLICES EACH)

- 1 **package white cake mix (regular size)**
- 1 **package (3.4 ounces) instant lemon pudding mix**
- 1 **cup warm water**
- 4 **eggs**
- ½ **cup canola oil**
- 4 **teaspoons poppy seeds**

1. Preheat oven to 350°. In a large bowl, combine cake mix, pudding mix, water, eggs and oil; beat on low speed 30 seconds. Beat on medium 2 minutes. Fold in poppy seeds.
2. Pour into two greased 9x5-in. loaf pans. Bake 35-40 minutes or until a toothpick inserted in center comes out clean. Cool in pans 10 minutes before removing to a wire rack.

WHITE CHOCOLATE MACADAMIA MUFFINS

Muffins are always a good choice for guests since they are so versatile and everyone likes them. These sweet muffins remind me of one of my favorite cookies. They're real kid-pleasers.

—**LORIE ROACH** BUCKATUNNA, MS

PREP: 20 MIN. • **BAKE:** 15 MIN.
MAKES: 1 DOZEN

- 1¾ cups all-purpose flour
- ¾ cup sugar
- 2½ teaspoons baking powder
- ½ teaspoon salt
- 1 egg
- ½ cup 2% milk
- ¼ cup butter, melted
- ¾ cup white baking chips
- ¾ cup chopped macadamia nuts

GLAZE
- ½ cup white baking chips
- 2 tablespoons heavy whipping cream

1. Preheat oven to 400°. In a large bowl, combine flour, sugar, baking powder and salt. In another bowl, combine egg, milk and butter; stir into dry ingredients just until moistened. Fold in chips and nuts.
2. Fill paper-lined muffin cups two-thirds full. Bake 15-18 minutes or until a toothpick inserted in the center comes out clean. Cool 5 minutes before removing from pan to a wire rack.
3. For glaze, in a microwave, melt chips with cream; stir until smooth. Drizzle over warm muffins. Serve warm.

BACON SCONES

I grew up in Scotland, where this scone was quite popular. It pairs perfectly with a salad.

—**TERESA ROYSTON** SEABECK, WA

PREP: 20 MIN. • **BAKE:** 15 MIN.
MAKES: 8 SCONES

- 1¾ cups all-purpose flour
- 2¼ teaspoons baking powder
- 1 teaspoon ground mustard
- ½ teaspoon salt
- ¼ teaspoon pepper
- 6 tablespoons cold butter
- 2 eggs
- ⅓ cup 2% milk
- ½ cup chopped onion
- ¼ cup shredded cheddar cheese
- 6 bacon strips, cooked and crumbled, divided

1. Preheat oven to 400°. In a large bowl, combine first five ingredients. Cut in butter until mixture resembles coarse crumbs. In a small bowl, whisk eggs and milk. Stir into dry ingredients just until moistened. Fold in onion, cheese and two-thirds of the bacon.
2. Transfer dough to a greased baking sheet. Pat into a 7½-in. circle. Cut into eight wedges, but do not separate. Sprinkle with remaining bacon. Bake 15-20 minutes or until golden brown. Serve warm.

BANANA CRUMB SNACK CAKE

Combining banana and almonds in this cake is a treat for your taste buds. Surprise the neighbors with a fresh-baked pan!

—GINA BUZZELL OGDEN, IA

PREP: 25 MIN. • **BAKE:** 35 MIN. + COOLING
MAKES: 12-16 SERVINGS

- ⅔ **cup slivered almonds**
- ¼ **cup packed brown sugar**
- ⅔ **cup butter, softened**
- 1½ **cups sugar**
- 2 **eggs**
- ¾ **teaspoon almond extract**
- 3 **cups all-purpose flour**
- 2 **teaspoons baking soda**
- ¼ **teaspoon baking powder**
- 2 **cups mashed ripe bananas (3 to 4 medium)**
- 1 **cup (8 ounces) sour cream**
- 1 **cup white baking chips**

1. Preheat oven to 350°. In a small bowl, combine almonds and brown sugar; set aside. In a large bowl, cream butter and sugar until light and fluffy. Add eggs, one at a time, beating well after each addition. Beat in extract.

2. Combine flour, baking soda and baking powder; add to the creamed mixture alternately with bananas and sour cream, beating well after each addition. Fold in chips.

3. Spread into a greased 13x9-in. baking pan. Sprinkle with reserved almond mixture. Bake 35-40 minutes or until a toothpick inserted near the center comes out clean. Cool in pan on a wire rack.

CHOCOLATE WALNUT RING

This is an adaptation of my wife's recipe. It's terrific for a special-occasion brunch or as a midmorning snack.

—PETER HALFERTY CORPUS CHRISTI, TX

PREP: 55 MIN. + RISING
BAKE: 20 MIN. + COOLING
MAKES: 18 20 SERVINGS

- 3 to 3½ cups all-purpose flour
- ¼ cup sugar
- 1 package (¼ ounce) active dry yeast
- 1 teaspoon ground cinnamon
- ½ teaspoon salt
- ½ cup milk
- ¼ cup water
- 2 tablespoons butter
- 2 tablespoons canola oil
- 1 egg
- 1 egg yolk

FILLING

- ½ cup miniature semisweet chocolate chips
- ½ cup chopped walnuts
- 3 tablespoons brown sugar

GLAZE

- ⅔ cup confectioners' sugar
- ⅛ teaspoon ground cinnamon
- ¼ teaspoon vanilla extract
- 3 to 4 teaspoons milk

1. In a large bowl, combine 1 cup flour, sugar, yeast, cinnamon and salt. In a small saucepan, heat milk, water, butter and oil to 120°-130°. Add to the dry ingredients; beat just until moistened. Add egg and yolk; beat until smooth. Stir in enough remaining flour to form a soft dough (dough will be sticky).

2. Turn onto a floured surface; knead until smooth and elastic, about 6-8 minutes. Place in a greased bowl, turning once to grease top. Cover and let rise in a warm place until doubled, about 1 hour. Combine the filling ingredients in a small bowl; set aside.

3. Punch dough down. Turn onto a lightly floured surface. Roll into an 18x9-in. rectangle; sprinkle with filling to within 1 in. of edges. Roll up tightly jelly-roll style, starting with a long side; seal ends.

4. Place seam side down on a greased 12-in. pizza pan; pinch ends together to form a ring. With scissors, cut from outside edge two-thirds of the way toward center of ring at 1-in. intervals. Separate strips slightly; twist to allow filling to show. Cover and let rise until doubled, about 40 minutes.

5. Preheat oven to 350°. Bake 18-22 minutes or until golden brown. Remove to a wire rack to cool completely. Mix glaze ingredients; drizzle over ring.

BRUNCH NOTES

CREAM CHEESE COFFEE CAKE

Here are impressive loaves that will really shine on the buffet. Everyone wants a second slice of this treat.

—MARY ANNE MCWHIRTER PEARLAND, TX

PREP: 35 MIN. + RISING
BAKE: 20 MIN. + COOLING
MAKES: 20-24 SERVINGS

- 1 cup (8 ounces) sour cream
- ½ cup sugar
- ½ cup butter, cubed
- 1 teaspoon salt
- 2 packages (¼ ounce each) active dry yeast
- ½ cup warm water (110° to 115°)
- 2 eggs, lightly beaten
- 4 cups all-purpose flour

FILLING

- 2 packages (8 ounces each) cream cheese, softened
- ¾ cup sugar
- 1 egg, lightly beaten
- 2 teaspoons vanilla extract
- ⅛ teaspoon salt

GLAZE

- 2½ cups confectioners' sugar
- ¼ cup milk
- 1 teaspoon vanilla extract
  Toasted sliced almonds, optional

1. In a small saucepan, combine sour cream, sugar, butter and salt. Cook over medium-low heat, stirring constantly, 5-10 minutes or until well blended. Cool to room temperature.

2. In a large bowl, dissolve yeast in warm water. Add sour cream mixture and eggs. Beat until smooth. Gradually stir in flour to form a soft dough (dough will be very soft). Cover and refrigerate overnight.

3. Punch dough down. Turn dough onto a floured surface; knead 5-6 times. Divide into fourths. Roll each piece into a 12x8-in. rectangle. In a large bowl, combine filling ingredients until well blended. Spread over each rectangle to within 1 in. of edges.

4. Roll up jelly-roll style, starting with a long side; pinch seams and ends to seal. Place seam side down on greased baking sheets. Cut six X's on top of loaves. Cover and let rise until nearly doubled, about 1 hour.

5. Preheat oven to 375°. Bake 20-25 minutes or until golden brown. Remove from pans to wire racks to cool. In a small bowl, combine confectioners' sugar, milk and vanilla; drizzle over warm loaves. If desired, sprinkle with almonds. Store in the refrigerator.

EASY MUFFIN PREP

You'll have extra time in the morning if you mix the dry ingredients for muffins in a plastic bag the night before. In the morning, combine the dry with the rest of the ingredients; stir and pop the muffins into the oven.

GLAZED LEMON BLUEBERRY MUFFINS

Bursting with berries and drizzled with a light lemony glaze, my muffins are moist, tender and truly something special. This is one recipe you simply must try for family and friends.

—KATHY HARDING RICHMOND, MO

PREP: 30 MIN. • **BAKE:** 25 MIN.
MAKES: 11 MUFFINS

- ½ **cup butter, softened**
- 1 **cup sugar**
- 2 **eggs**
- ½ **cup 2% milk**
- 2 **tablespoons lemon juice**
- 2 **teaspoons grated lemon peel**
- 2 **cups all-purpose flour**
- 2 **teaspoons baking powder**
  Dash salt
- 2 **cups fresh or frozen blueberries**

GLAZE

- 1½ **cups confectioners' sugar**
- 2 **tablespoons lemon juice**
- 1 **teaspoon butter, melted**
- ¼ **teaspoon vanilla extract**

1. Preheat oven to 400°. In a large bowl, cream butter and sugar until light and fluffy. Add eggs, one at a time, beating well after each addition. Beat in milk, lemon juice and peel. Combine flour, baking powder and salt; add to creamed mixture just until moistened. Fold in blueberries.

2. Fill paper-lined regular-size muffin cups three-fourths full. Bake 25-30 minutes or until a toothpick inserted in muffin comes out clean. Cool 5 minutes; remove from pan to a wire rack.

3. In a small bowl, mix confectioners' sugar, lemon juice, butter and vanilla; drizzle over warm muffins.

NOTE *If using frozen blueberries, use without thawing to avoid discoloring the batter.*

STICKY BUNS

It's impossible to eat just one of these soft, yummy sticky buns—they have wonderful old-fashioned goodness.

—DOROTHY SHOWALTER BROADWAY, VA

PREP: 30 MIN. + RISING
BAKE: 20 MIN. + COOLING
MAKES: 1 DOZEN

- **2 teaspoons active dry yeast**
- **1¼ cups warm water (110° to 115°)**
- **3 tablespoons butter, softened**
- **3 tablespoons sugar**
- **2 tablespoons nonfat dry milk powder**
- **1 teaspoon salt**
- **3 to 3¼ cups bread flour**

FILLING
- **⅓ cup butter, softened**
- **1 tablespoon sugar**
- **1 teaspoon ground cinnamon**

SAUCE
- **½ cup packed brown sugar**
- **¼ cup butter, cubed**
- **¼ cup corn syrup**
- **½ cup chopped pecans**

1. In a large bowl, dissolve yeast in water. Add butter, sugar, milk powder, salt and 2 cups flour; beat on low speed 3 minutes. Stir in enough remaining flour to form a soft dough.

2. Turn onto a floured surface; knead until smooth and elastic, about 6-8 minutes. Place in a greased bowl; turn once to grease top. Cover and let rise in a warm place until doubled, about 1 hour.

3. Punch dough down. Roll dough into a 16x10-in. rectangle. Spread with softened butter; sprinkle with sugar and cinnamon. Roll up from a long side; pinch seam to seal. Cut into 12 slices; set aside.

4. In a small saucepan, combine brown sugar, butter and corn syrup; cook over medium heat until the sugar is dissolved. Stir in pecans. Pour into a greased 13x9-in. baking dish. Place slices cut side down over sauce. Cover and let rise until doubled, about 1 hour.

5. Preheat oven to 375°. Bake 20-25 minutes or until golden brown. Cool 3 minutes before inverting onto a serving platter.

NOTE *The dough may be prepared in a bread machine. Place dough ingredients (using water that is 70°-80° and only 3 cups of bread flour) in bread pan in order suggested by manufacturer. Select dough setting (check dough after 5 minutes of mixing; add 1-2 tablespoons of water or flour if needed). When cycle is completed, turn dough onto a floured surface and punch down. Prepare buns as directed.*

APPLE FRITTERS

My kids love these fritters year-round, but I get even more requests in the fall when apples are abundantly in season. I like to serve the fritters as a special breakfast treat when the kids host friends for sleepovers.

—KATIE BEECHY SEYMOUR, MO

PREP: 15 MIN. • **COOK:** 5 MIN./BATCH
MAKES: 40 FRITTERS

- **2½ cups all-purpose flour**
- **½ cup nonfat dry milk powder**
- **⅓ cup sugar**
- **2 teaspoons baking powder**
- **1 teaspoon salt**
- **2 eggs**
- **1 cup water**
- **2 cups chopped peeled apples**
  Oil for deep-fat frying
  Sugar

1. In a large bowl, combine the first five ingredients. Whisk eggs and water; add to dry ingredients just until moistened. Fold in apples.

2. In an electric skillet, heat oil to 375°. Drop batter by tablespoonfuls, a few at a time, into hot oil. Fry until golden brown, about 1½ minutes on each side. Drain on paper towels. Roll warm fritters in sugar. Serve warm.

TENDER LEMON ROLLS

Light and tender, these golden rolls are filled with a lemon curd sauce and are glazed with a lemony topping. Whether or not you add a sprinkle of walnuts, this sweet roll is hard to resist.

—SHIRLEY DUNCAN WILLIS, VA

PREP: 30 MIN. + RISING • **BAKE:** 25 MIN.
MAKES: 1 DOZEN

- 2½ to 3 cups all-purpose flour
- ⅓ cup sugar
- 1 tablespoon active dry yeast
- ½ teaspoon grated lemon peel
- ¼ teaspoon salt
- ½ cup sour cream
- ⅓ cup butter, cubed
- ¼ cup water
- 2 eggs
- ¾ cup lemon curd
- 1 egg, lightly beaten
- ½ cup chopped walnuts, optional

ICING
- ½ cup confectioners' sugar
- 1 teaspoon water
- 1 teaspoon lemon juice
- ¼ teaspoon grated lemon peel

1. In a large bowl, combine 1½ cups flour, sugar, yeast, lemon peel and salt. In a small saucepan, heat sour cream, butter and water to 120°-130°; add to dry ingredients. Beat on medium speed 2 minutes. Add eggs and ½ cup flour; beat 2 minutes longer. Stir in enough remaining flour to form a soft dough (dough will be sticky).

2. Turn dough onto a floured surface; knead until smooth and elastic, about 6-8 minutes. Place in a greased bowl, turning once to grease the top. Cover and let rise in a warm place until doubled, about 1 hour.

3. Punch dough down; turn onto a floured surface. Roll into an 18x12-in. rectangle. Spread lemon curd to within ½ in. of edges. Roll up jelly-roll style, starting with a long side; pinch seams to seal. Cut into 12 slices.

4. Place rolls, cut side down, in a greased 13x9-in. baking dish. Cover and let rise until doubled, about 30 minutes.

5. Preheat oven to 350°. Brush rolls with beaten egg and, if desired, sprinkle with walnuts. Bake 25-30 minutes or until golden brown.

6. In a small bowl, combine icing ingredients; drizzle over warm rolls.

Raspberry Almond
Coffee Cake

RASPBERRY ALMOND COFFEE CAKE

Raspberries and almonds lift this coffee cake to a tart and nutty place.

—DEBBIE JOHNSON JEFFERSON CITY, MO

PREP: 20 MIN. • **BAKE:** 30 MIN. + COOLING
MAKES: 8 SERVINGS

- 1 **cup fresh raspberries**
- 3 **tablespoons brown sugar**
- 1 **cup all-purpose flour**
- ⅓ **cup sugar**
- ½ **teaspoon baking powder**
- ¼ **teaspoon baking soda**
- ⅛ **teaspoon salt**
- 1 **egg**
- ½ **cup sour cream**
- 3 **tablespoons butter, melted**
- 1 **teaspoon vanilla extract**
- ¼ **cup sliced almonds**

ICING

- ¼ **cup confectioners' sugar**
- 1½ **teaspoons 2% milk**
- ¼ **teaspoon vanilla extract**

1. Preheat oven to 350°. In a small bowl, combine raspberries and brown sugar; set aside.

2. In a large bowl, combine flour, sugar, baking powder, baking soda and salt. In a small bowl, whisk egg, sour cream, butter and vanilla. Stir into the dry ingredients just until moistened.

3. Spoon half of batter into a greased and floured 8-in. round baking pan. Top with raspberry mixture. Spoon remaining batter over raspberries; sprinkle with almonds.

4. Bake 30-35 minutes or until a toothpick inserted near the center comes out clean. Cool 10 minutes; remove from pan to a wire rack. In a small bowl, combine icing ingredients; drizzle over coffee cake. Serve warm.

LONG JOHNS

The tattered recipe in my files is a good indication of how popular these doughnuts have been in our family over the years. They disappear in a hurry, so I typically double the recipe.

—TWILLA EISELE WELLSVILLE, KS

PREP: 15 MIN. + RISING
COOK: 5 MIN./BATCH • **MAKES:** 2½ DOZEN

- 1 **package (¼ ounce) active dry yeast**
- ¼ **cup warm water (110° to 115°)**
- 1 **cup warm milk (110° to 115°)**
- ¼ **cup butter, softened**
- ¼ **cup sugar**
- ½ **teaspoon salt**
- 1 **egg**
- 3¼ **to 3¾ cups all-purpose flour**
  Oil for deep-fat frying

GLAZE
- 1¼ **cups confectioners' sugar**
- 1 **tablespoon brown sugar**
- 1 **tablespoon water**
- ½ **teaspoon vanilla extract**
- ⅛ **teaspoon salt**

1. In a large bowl, dissolve yeast in warm water. Add milk, butter, sugar, salt and egg and 2 cups flour. Beat until smooth. Stir in enough flour to form a soft dough.
2. Do not knead. Place in a greased bowl, turning once to grease top. Cover and let the dough rise in a warm place until doubled, about 1 hour.
3. Punch dough down. Turn onto a lightly floured surface; roll into a 12x8-in. rectangle. Cut into 3x1-in. rectangles. Place on greased baking sheets. Cover and let rise in a warm place until doubled, about 30 minutes.
4. In an electric skillet or deep-fat fryer, heat oil to 400°. Fry doughnuts, a few at a time, until golden brown on both sides. Drain on paper towels. Combine glaze ingredients. Dip tops in glaze while warm.

WALNUT PASTRY ROLLS

These are incredible served warm with a little bit of butter spread on top, and they reheat well. The rolls are tasty either plain or frosted for some extra sweetness.

—DIANE TURNER BRUNSWICK, OH

PREP: 2 HOURS + CHILLING
BAKE: 20 MIN. + COOLING
MAKES: 4 ROLLS (15 SLICES EACH)

- 1½ cups plus ⅓ cup sugar, divided
- 1 can (12 ounces) evaporated milk, divided
- 6 cups ground walnuts (1½ pounds)
- 1½ teaspoons honey
- 3 eggs, separated
- 2 packages (¼ ounce each) active dry yeast
- ¾ cup warm water (110° to 115°)
- 4 to 4½ cups all-purpose flour
- 1 teaspoon salt
- ½ cup cold butter, cubed
- 3 to 4 tablespoons milk, divided
- 1 to 2 cups confectioners' sugar

1. In a small saucepan, cook and stir 1½ cups sugar and 1 cup evaporated milk until the mixture comes to a boil. Transfer to a large bowl; stir in walnuts and honey. In a small bowl, beat the egg whites until stiff peaks form. Fold into walnut mixture. Cover and refrigerate filling at least 2 hours.

2. For dough, in a small bowl, dissolve yeast in warm water. In a large bowl, mix 3 cups flour, salt and remaining sugar; cut in butter until crumbly. Add yeast mixture, egg yolks and remaining evaporated milk; beat until smooth. Stir in enough remaining flour to form a firm dough.

3. Turn dough onto a floured surface; knead until smooth and elastic, about

6-8 minutes. Place dough in a greased bowl, turning once to grease the top. Cover and let the dough rise in a warm place until doubled, about 1 hour.

4. Turn onto a floured surface. Punch dough down; divide into four portions. Roll each portion into a 15x11-in. rectangle. Spread the walnut filling to within ½ in. of edges. Roll up jelly-roll style, starting with a long side; pinch seams to seal and tuck ends under. Place seam side down on greased baking sheets. Cover and let rise in a warm place until doubled, about 30 minutes.

5. Meanwhile, preheat oven to 350°. Brush 2 tablespoons milk over tops and sides of rolls. Bake 20-25 minutes or until golden brown. Cool on wire racks.

6. Combine the confectioners' sugar and enough remaining milk to achieve desired consistency; drizzle over the warm rolls.

STORING YEAST

Unopened packages of dry yeast should be stored in a cool, dark, dry place and used by the "best if used by" date on the package. Opened packages or bulk dry yeast should be stored in an airtight container in the refrigerator for about 6 weeks or frozen for up to 6 months.

_____

_____

_____

_____

_____

_____

_____

_____

_____

_____

_____

_____

_____

_____

_____

_____

_____

_____

_____

_____

_____

_____

_____

_____

_____

_____

_____

_____

_____

_____

BLUEBERRY SOUR CREAM COFFEE CAKE

Special-occasion breakfasts would not be the same at our house without this delectable coffee cake.

—SUSAN WALSCHLAGER ANDERSON, IN

PREP: 25 MIN. • **BAKE:** 55 MIN. + COOLING
MAKES: 10-12 SERVINGS

- ¾ cup butter, softened
- 1½ cups sugar
- 4 eggs
- 1 teaspoon vanilla extract
- 3 cups all-purpose flour
- 1½ teaspoons baking powder
- ¾ teaspoon baking soda
- ¼ teaspoon salt
- 1 cup (8 ounces) sour cream

FILLING

- ¼ cup packed brown sugar
- 1 tablespoon all-purpose flour
- ½ teaspoon ground cinnamon
- 2 cups fresh or frozen blueberries

GLAZE

- 1 cup confectioners' sugar
- 2 to 3 tablespoons 2% milk

1. Preheat oven to 350°. In a large bowl, cream butter and sugar until light and fluffy. Add eggs, one at a time, beating well after each addition. Beat in vanilla. Mix flour, baking powder, baking soda and salt; add to creamed mixture alternately with sour cream, beating well after each addition.

2. Spoon a third of the batter into a greased and floured 10-in. tube pan. Combine brown sugar, flour and cinnamon; sprinkle half over batter. Top with half of the berries. Repeat layers. Top with remaining batter.

3. Bake 55-65 minutes or until a toothpick inserted in center comes out clean. Cool 10 minutes; remove from pan to a wire rack to cool completely. Mix glaze ingredients; drizzle over warm coffee cake.

NOTE *If using frozen blueberries, use without thawing to avoid discoloring the batter.*

Blueberry Sour Cream
Coffee Cake

RASPBERRY STREUSEL COFFEE CAKE

One of my mother's friends used to bring this over on holidays, and it never lasted long. With the tangy raspberry filling and crunchy topping, it's a favorite at our house.

—**AMY MITCHELL** SABETHA, KS

PREP: 25 MIN. + COOLING • **BAKE:** 40 MIN.
MAKES: 12-16 SERVINGS

- 3½ cups unsweetened raspberries
- 1 cup water
- 2 tablespoons lemon juice
- 1¼ cups sugar
- ⅓ cup cornstarch

BATTER

- 3 cups all-purpose flour
- 1 cup sugar
- 1 teaspoon baking powder
- 1 teaspoon baking soda
- 1 cup cold butter, cubed
- 2 eggs, lightly beaten
- 1 cup (8 ounces) sour cream
- 1 teaspoon vanilla extract

TOPPING

- ½ cup all-purpose flour
- ½ cup sugar
- ¼ cup butter, softened
- ½ cup chopped pecans

GLAZE

- ½ cup confectioners' sugar
- 2 teaspoons 2% milk
- ½ teaspoon vanilla extract

1. In a large saucepan, cook raspberries and water over medium heat 5 minutes. Add lemon juice. Combine sugar and cornstarch; stir into fruit mixture. Bring to a boil; cook and stir 2 minutes or until thickened. Cool.

2. Preheat oven to 350°. In a large bowl, combine flour, sugar, baking powder and baking soda. Cut in butter until mixture resembles coarse crumbs. Stir in eggs, sour cream and vanilla (batter will be stiff).

3. Spread half into a greased 13x9-in. baking dish. Spread raspberry filling over batter; spoon remaining batter over filling. Mix topping ingredients; sprinkle over top.

4. Bake 40-45 minutes or until golden brown. Combine the glaze ingredients; drizzle over warm cake.

COFFEE-GLAZED DOUGHNUTS

The coffee-flavored glaze on these moist and tasty doughnuts makes them a perfect way to start off the morning. You'll find that this recipe is a smart way to use up leftover potatoes.

—PAT SIEBENALER RANDOM LAKE, WI

PREP: 25 MIN. + RISING
COOK: 5 MIN./BATCH
MAKES: ABOUT 4 DOZEN

- 2   **packages (¼ ounce each) active dry yeast**
- ¼   **cup warm water (110° to 115°)**
- 2   **cups warm 2% milk (110° to 115°)**
- ½   **cup butter, softened**
- 1   **cup hot mashed potatoes (without added milk and butter)**
- 3   **eggs**
- ½   **teaspoon lemon extract, optional**
- 1   **cup sugar**
- 1½ **teaspoons salt**
- ½   **teaspoon ground cinnamon**
- 9¼ to 9¾ **cups all-purpose flour**

COFFEE GLAZE
- 6   **to 8 tablespoons cold 2% milk**
- 1   **tablespoon instant coffee granules**
- 2   **teaspoons vanilla extract**
- ¾   **cup butter, softened**
- 6   **cups confectioners' sugar**
- ½   **teaspoon ground cinnamon**
     Dash salt
     Oil for deep-fat frying

1. In a large bowl, dissolve yeast in warm water. Add milk, butter, potatoes, eggs and, if desired, extract. Add sugar, salt, cinnamon and 3 cups flour. Beat until smooth. Stir in enough remaining flour to form a soft dough. Cover and let rise in a warm place until doubled, about 1 hour.

2. Stir down dough. On a well-floured surface, roll out to ½-in. thickness. Cut with a floured 2½-in. doughnut cutter. Place on greased baking sheets; cover and let rise for 45 minutes.

3. Meanwhile, for the glaze, combine 6 tablespoons milk, coffee and vanilla; stir to dissolve coffee. In a large bowl, beat the butter, sugar, cinnamon and salt. Gradually add milk mixture; beat until smooth, adding additional milk to make a dipping consistency.

4. In an electric skillet or deep-fat fryer, heat oil to 375°. Fry doughnuts, a few at a time, about 1½ minutes per side or until golden. Drain on paper towels. Dip tops in glaze while warm.

GOLDEN DANISH TWISTS

Graceful, beautiful rolls have a rich filling, crunchy almonds and sweet, lemony icing. They would be lovely any day of the year.
—**ANNIE DE LA HOZ** DELTA, CO

PREP: 1¼ HOURS + RISING • **BAKE:** 15 MIN.
MAKES: 3 DOZEN

- 2 **packages (¼ ounce each) active dry yeast**
- ½ **cup warm water (110° to 115°)**
- 1 **cup canned pumpkin**
- 1 **cup warm 2% milk (110° to 115°)**
- 2 **eggs**
- ¼ **cup sugar**
- ¼ **cup butter, softened**
- 3 **teaspoons salt**
- 6 **to 6½ cups all-purpose flour**

FILLING

- 2 **packages (8 ounces each) cream cheese, softened**
- ⅓ **cup confectioners' sugar**
- ½ **cup heavy whipping cream**
- 2 **teaspoons grated lemon peel**
- 1 **teaspoon vanilla extract**

ICING

- ¼ **cup butter, cubed**
- 2 **tablespoons all-purpose flour**
- ¼ **cup lemon juice**
- 2⅔ **cups confectioners' sugar**
- 1 **tablespoon grated lemon peel**
- ¾ **cup sliced almonds**

1. In a small bowl, dissolve yeast in warm water. In a large bowl, combine the pumpkin, milk, eggs, sugar, butter, salt, yeast mixture and 3 cups flour; beat on medium speed until smooth. Stir in enough of the remaining flour to make a soft dough.

2. Turn dough onto a floured surface; knead until smooth and elastic, about 6-8 minutes. Place in a greased bowl, turning once to grease the top. Cover with plastic wrap and let rise in a warm place until doubled, about 1 hour.

3. For filling, in a small bowl, beat the cream cheese and confectioners' sugar until smooth. Gradually beat in cream, lemon peel and vanilla.

4. Punch down dough. Turn onto a lightly floured surface. Divide dough in half. Roll one portion into an 18x12-in. rectangle. Spread half of the filling lengthwise down half of the dough to within ½ in. of edges. Fold dough over filling; seal edges. Cut into eighteen 1-in. strips. Twist and loosely coil each strip; tuck end under and pinch to seal.

5. Place 2 in. apart on greased baking sheets. Cover and let rise in a warm place until doubled, about 30 minutes. Repeat with the remaining dough and filling.

6. Preheat oven to 375°. Bake twists 12-15 minutes or until golden brown. Remove to wire racks.

7. For icing, in a large saucepan, melt butter. Stir in flour until smooth. Stir in lemon juice. Bring to a boil; cook and stir 2 minutes or until the mixture is thickened. Remove from heat. Stir in the confectioners' sugar and lemon peel until blended. Drizzle over the warm twists. Sprinkle with the almonds. Refrigerate leftovers.

PECAN APPLE STRUDEL

This is one of my favorite recipes to make during autumn. The aroma of homemade strudel baking on a cool, crisp day is absolutely wonderful.

—HELEN LESH FORSYTH, MO

PREP: 20 MIN. + CHILLING
BAKE: 55 MIN. + COOLING
MAKES: 3 STRUDELS (12 SLICES EACH)

- 1 **cup cold butter, cubed**
- 2 **cups all-purpose flour**
- 1 **cup (8 ounces) sour cream**
- ¼ **teaspoon salt**

FILLING

- 2 **cups dry bread crumbs**
- ¼ **cup butter, melted**
- 4 **medium tart apples, peeled and chopped**
- 2 **cups sugar**
- 1 **cup golden raisins**
- ½ **cup chopped pecans**
- 2 **teaspoons ground cinnamon**
  Confectioners' sugar, optional

1. In a large bowl, cut the butter into flour until mixture resembles coarse crumbs. Stir in the sour cream and salt. Shape the dough into a ball; cover and refrigerate overnight.

2. For filling, combine bread crumbs and butter. Add apples, sugar, raisins, pecans and cinnamon; set aside.

3. Preheat oven to 350°. Divide dough into thirds; turn onto a floured surface. Roll each into a 15x12-in. rectangle. Spoon filling evenly onto dough; spread to within 1 in. of edges. Roll up from a long side; pinch seams and ends to seal.

4. Carefully place each loaf seam side down on an ungreased baking sheet. Bake 55-60 minutes or until strudels are lightly browned. Cool completely on wire racks. Dust with confectioners' sugar if desired.

MORNING MAPLE MUFFINS

Maple combines with a subtle touch of cinnamon and nuts to give these muffins the flavor of a hearty pancake breakfast.

—ELIZABETH TALBOT LEXINGTON, KY

START TO FINISH: 30 MIN.
MAKES: 16 MUFFINS

- 2 **cups all-purpose flour**
- ½ **cup packed brown sugar**
- 2 **teaspoons baking powder**
- ½ **teaspoon salt**
- ¾ **cup milk**
- ½ **cup butter, melted**
- ½ **cup maple syrup**
- ¼ **cup sour cream**
- 1 **egg**
- ½ **teaspoon vanilla extract**

TOPPING

- 3 **tablespoons all-purpose flour**
- 3 **tablespoons sugar**
- 2 **tablespoons chopped nuts**
- ½ **teaspoon ground cinnamon**
- 2 **tablespoons cold butter**

1. Preheat oven to 400°. In a large bowl, combine flour, brown sugar, baking powder and salt. In another bowl, combine milk, butter, syrup, sour cream, egg and vanilla. Stir into dry ingredients just until moistened.

2. Fill greased or paper-lined muffin cups two-thirds full. For the topping, combine the flour, sugar, nuts and cinnamon; cut in butter until crumbly. Sprinkle over batter.

3. Bake 16-20 minutes or until a toothpick inserted in center comes out clean. Cool 5 minutes before removing from pans to wire racks. Serve warm.

APRICOT BRAIDS

These lovely yeast braids are tender and light. Their delightful apricot filling makes them very popular with everyone.

—PAULA WIPF ARLINGTON, VA

PREP: 1 HOUR + RISING
BAKE: 20 MIN. + COOLING
MAKES: 3 BRAIDS

- 2¼ cups chopped dried apricots
- 1½ cups water, divided
- 1½ cups packed brown sugar
- 5½ to 6 cups all-purpose flour
- ¾ cup sugar
- 3 packages (¼ ounce each) active dry yeast
- 1 teaspoon salt
- ½ cup butter, softened
- 3 eggs, beaten

GLAZE
- 1 cup confectioners' sugar
- 1 to 2 tablespoons milk
- ½ teaspoon vanilla extract

1. In a saucepan, bring apricots and ½ cup water to a boil. Reduce heat; cover and simmer until the water is absorbed and the apricots are tender, about 20 minutes. Transfer to a food processor; add brown sugar. Cover and process until smooth.

2. In a bowl, combine 2 cups of flour, sugar, yeast and salt. In a saucepan, heat butter and remaining water to 120°-130°. Add to dry ingredients; beat just until moistened. Add the eggs; beat until smooth. Stir in enough remaining flour to form a soft dough.

3. Turn dough onto a floured surface; knead until smooth and elastic, about 6-8 minutes. Place in a greased bowl, turning once to grease top. Cover and let rise in a warm place until doubled, about 40-45 minutes.

4. Punch dough down; divide into thirds. On greased baking sheets, roll out each portion of dough into a 12x8-in. rectangle. Spread filling down the center of each rectangle. On each long side, cut 1-in.-wide strips about 2 in. into center. Starting at one end, fold alternating strips at an angle across filling. Pinch ends to seal. Cover and let rise for 30 minutes.

5. Preheat oven to 375°. Bake 20-25 minutes or until golden brown. Remove from the pans to wire racks to cool. Combine the glaze ingredients; drizzle over braids.

BRUNCH NOTES

BUTTERMILK ANGEL BISCUITS

When I make these slightly sweet biscuits, sometimes I cut them and fold over one side about a third of the way for a more traditional look.

—**CAROL HOLLADAY** DANVILLE, AL

PREP: 30 MIN. + STANDING
BAKE: 10 MIN. • **MAKES:** 2 DOZEN

- 2 packages (¼ ounce each) active dry yeast
- ¼ cup warm water (110° to 115°)
- 5¼ to 5½ cups self-rising flour
- ⅓ cup sugar
- 1 teaspoon baking soda
- 1 cup shortening
- 1¾ cups buttermilk

1. In a small bowl, dissolve yeast in warm water. In a large bowl, whisk 5¼ cups flour, sugar and baking soda. Cut in shortening until mixture resembles coarse crumbs. Stir in buttermilk and yeast mixture to form a soft dough (dough will be sticky).
2. Turn onto a floured surface; knead gently 8-10 times, adding additional flour if needed. Roll dough to ¾-in. thickness; cut with a floured 2½-in. biscuit cutter. Place 2 in. apart on greased baking sheets. Let stand at room temperature 20 minutes. Preheat oven to 450°.
3. Bake 8-12 minutes or until golden brown. Serve warm.

CHERRY CHIP SCONES

These buttery scones, dotted with dried cherries and white chips, are so delicious and flaky that I will even serve them for dessert.

—**PAMELA BROOKS** SOUTH BERWICK, ME

PREP: 15 MIN. • **BAKE:** 20 MIN.
MAKES: 8 SERVINGS

- 3 cups all-purpose flour
- ½ cup sugar
- 2½ teaspoons baking powder
- ½ teaspoon baking soda
- 6 tablespoons cold butter
- 1 cup (8 ounces) vanilla yogurt
- ¼ cup plus 2 tablespoons milk, divided
- 1⅓ cups dried cherries
- ⅔ cup white baking chips
  Coarse sugar, optional

1. Preheat oven to 400°. In a large bowl, combine flour, sugar, baking powder and baking soda. Cut in butter until the mixture resembles coarse crumbs. Combine yogurt and ¼ cup milk; stir into crumb mixture just until moistened. Knead in cherries and chips.
2. On a greased baking sheet, pat dough into a 9-in. circle. Cut into eight wedges; separate wedges. Brush with remaining milk. If desired, sprinkle with sugar. Bake 20-25 minutes or until golden brown. Serve warm.

Cherry Chip
Scones

CLASSIC FRUIT KOLACHES

PREP: 35 MIN. + RISING
BAKE: 15 MIN./BATCH
MAKES: 2½ DOZEN

- 6 **to 7 cups all-purpose flour**
- ¼ **cup sugar**
- 2 **packages (¼ ounce each) active dry yeast**
- 2 **teaspoons salt**
- 2 **cups 2% milk**
- ½ **cup butter, cubed**
- ½ **cup water**
- 6 **egg yolks**
- ¼ **cup butter, melted**
- 1 **can (12 ounces) raspberry and/or apricot cake and pastry filling**

ICING

- 3 **cups confectioners' sugar**
- ¼ **cup butter, softened**
- 2 **teaspoons vanilla extract**
- ½ **teaspoon salt**
- 4 **to 6 tablespoons 2% milk**

1. In a large bowl, combine 3 cups flour, sugar, yeast and salt. In a large saucepan, heat the milk, cubed butter and water to 120°-130°. Add to the dry ingredients; beat just until moistened. Add egg yolks; beat until smooth. Stir in enough remaining flour to form a soft dough (dough will be sticky). Do not knead. Cover and let rise until doubled, about 45 minutes.

2. Turn dough onto a floured surface; roll to ½-in. thickness. Cut with a floured 2½-in. biscuit cutter. Place 2 in. apart on lightly greased baking sheets. Brush with melted butter. Cover and let rise in a warm place until doubled, about 30 minutes.

3. Preheat oven to 350°. Using the back of a spoon, make an indentation in the center of each roll. Spoon a heaping teaspoonful of raspberry and/or apricot filling into each indentation. Bake 15-20 minutes or until golden brown. Remove from pans to wire racks to cool.

4. Combine confectioners' sugar, butter, vanilla, salt and enough milk to achieve desired consistency. Drizzle over rolls.

NOTE *This recipe was tested with Solo brand cake and pastry filling. Look for it in the baking aisle.*

> We love making these melt-in-your-mouth goodies. For extra fun, use cookie cutters instead of a biscuit cutter.
>
> —GLEN & SUE ELLEN BORKHOLDER STURGIS, MI

OVERNIGHT CHERRY DANISH

Try my Danish. The rolls have cherry-filled centers and will melt in your mouth. Plus, they store well, unfrosted, in the freezer.
—LEANN SAUDER TREMONT, IL

PREP: 1½ HOURS + CHILLING
BAKE: 15 MIN. + COOLING
MAKES: 3 DOZEN

- 2 packages (¼ ounce each) active dry yeast
- ½ cup warm 2% milk (110° to 115°)
- 6 cups all-purpose flour
- ⅓ cup sugar
- 2 teaspoons salt
- 1 cup cold butter, cubed
- 1½ cups warm half-and-half cream (70° to 80°)
- 6 egg yolks
- 1 can (21 ounces) cherry pie filling

ICING
- 3 cups confectioners' sugar
- 2 tablespoons butter, softened
- ¼ teaspoon vanilla extract
  Dash salt
- 4 to 5 tablespoons half-and-half cream

1. In a small bowl, dissolve yeast in warm milk. In a large bowl, combine flour, sugar and salt. Cut in butter until crumbly. Add yeast mixture, cream and egg yolks; stir until mixture forms a soft dough (dough will be sticky). Refrigerate, covered, overnight.

2. Punch down the dough. Turn onto a lightly floured surface; divide into four portions. Roll each portion of dough into an 18x4-in. rectangle; cut into 4x1-in. strips.

   Place two strips side by side; twist together. Shape each twist into a ring and pinch ends together. Place 2 in. apart on greased baking sheets. Repeat with remaining strips. Cover and let rise in a warm place until doubled, about 45 minutes.

3. Preheat oven to 350°. Using the end of a wooden spoon handle, make a ½-in.-deep indentation in the center of each Danish. Fill each roll with about 1 tablespoon pie filling. Bake 14-16 minutes or until lightly browned. Remove from pans to wire racks to cool.

4. For icing, combine confectioners' sugar, butter, vanilla, salt and enough cream to reach desired consistency. Drizzle over Danish.

BRUNCH NOTES

Broccoli-Ham
Bake

Hot from
the Oven

BROCCOLI-HAM BAKE

A very dear friend shared this dish with me. My family loves it because it includes one of our favorite vegetables—broccoli. It's a delicious and colorful way to use up leftover ham.

—MARGARET ALLEN ABINGDON, VA

PREP: 20 MIN. • **BAKE:** 30 MIN.
MAKES: 8 SERVINGS

- 2 packages (10 ounces each) frozen cut broccoli
- 2 cups cooked rice
- 6 tablespoons butter, cubed
- 2 cups fresh bread crumbs (about 2½ slices)
- 1 medium onion, chopped
- 3 tablespoons all-purpose flour
- 1 teaspoon salt
- ¼ teaspoon pepper
- 3 cups milk
- 1½ pounds fully cooked ham, cubed
  Shredded cheddar or Swiss cheese

1. Preheat oven to 350°. Cook broccoli according to package directions; drain. Spoon rice into a 13x9-in. baking pan. Place broccoli over rice.
2. Melt the butter in a large skillet. Sprinkle 2 tablespoons of melted butter over the bread crumbs and set aside. Saute onion in remaining butter until soft. Add flour, salt and pepper, stirring constantly until blended; gradually stir in milk. Bring to a boil; cook and stir 2 minutes or until thickened. Add ham.
3. Pour over rice and broccoli. Sprinkle with crumbs. Bake 30 minutes or until heated through. Sprinkle with cheese; let stand 5 minutes before serving.

CHURCH SUPPER HOT DISH

This recipe was in my mother's church cookbook, and now it's in my church cookbook! Apparently it was too good to skip a generation. I often make this dish to take along to potlucks.

—NORMA TURNER HASLETT, MI

PREP: 40 MIN. • **BAKE:** 30 MIN.
MAKES: 8 SERVINGS

- 1 pound ground beef
- 2 cups sliced peeled potatoes
- 2 cups finely chopped celery
- ¾ cup finely chopped carrots
- ¼ cup finely chopped green pepper
- ¼ cup finely chopped onion
- 2 tablespoons butter
- 1 cup water
- 2 cans (10¾ ounces each) condensed cream of mushroom soup, undiluted
- 1 can (5 ounces) chow mein noodles, divided
- 1 cup (4 ounces) shredded cheddar cheese

1. Preheat oven to 350°. In a large skillet, cook beef over medium heat until no longer pink; drain and set aside.
2. In same skillet, saute potatoes, celery, carrots, green pepper and onion in butter for 5 minutes. Add the water; cover and simmer 10 minutes or until vegetables are tender. Stir in soup and cooked ground beef until blended.
3. Sprinkle half of the chow mein noodles into a greased shallow 2-qt. baking dish. Spoon the meat mixture over noodles.
4. Cover and bake 20 minutes. Top with cheese and remaining noodles. Bake, uncovered, 10 minutes longer or until heated through.

CHICKEN LASAGNA ROLLS

Whether for an everyday meal or a special occasion, this is a fun and creative way to serve lasagna. Chicken and almonds add a tasty twist.

—VIRGINIA SHAW MODESTO, CA

PREP: 45 MIN. • **BAKE:** 25 MIN.
MAKES: 5 SERVINGS

- 1 **medium onion, chopped**
- ½ **cup chopped sweet red pepper**
- ½ **cup chopped almonds**
- ⅓ **cup butter**
- ½ **cup cornstarch**
- 1½ **teaspoons salt**
- 2 **cans (10½ ounces each) condensed chicken broth, undiluted**
- 2 **cups chopped cooked chicken**
- 1 **package (10 ounces) frozen chopped spinach, thawed and well drained**
- ¼ **teaspoon pepper**
- ¼ **teaspoon ground nutmeg**
- 10 **lasagna noodles, cooked and drained**
- 2 **cups milk**
- 1 **cup (4 ounces) shredded Swiss cheese, divided**
- ¼ **cup dry white wine or water**

1. Preheat oven to 350°. In a large saucepan, saute onion, red pepper and almonds in butter until onion is tender and almonds are toasted. Stir in cornstarch and salt until blended. Stir in broth. Bring to a boil; cook and stir 2 minutes or until thickened.
2. Transfer half of the sauce to a large bowl; stir in the chicken, spinach, pepper and nutmeg. Spread about 3 tablespoons over each lasagna noodle. Roll up and place seam side down in a greased 11x7-in. baking dish.
3. Add milk, ½ cup Swiss cheese and wine to remaining sauce. Cook and stir over medium heat until thickened and bubbly. Pour over roll-ups.
4. Bake, uncovered, 20-25 minutes. Sprinkle with the remaining cheese; bake 5 minutes longer or until the cheese is melted.

SAUSAGE SANDWICH SQUARES

PREP: 35 MIN. + RISING • **BAKE:** 20 MIN.
MAKES: 12-15 SERVINGS

- 1 package (¼ ounce) active dry yeast
- 1⅓ cups warm water (110° to 115°), divided
- ½ teaspoon salt
- 3 to 3½ cups all-purpose flour
- 1 pound bulk Italian sausage
- 1 medium sweet red pepper, diced
- 1 medium green pepper, diced
- 1 large onion, diced
- 4 cups (16 ounces) shredded part-skim mozzarella cheese
- 1 egg
- 1 tablespoon water
- 2 tablespoons grated Parmesan cheese
- 2 tablespoons minced fresh parsley
- ½ teaspoon dried oregano
- ⅛ teaspoon garlic powder

1. In a large bowl, dissolve yeast in ½ cup warm water. Add the salt, remaining water and 2 cups flour. Beat until smooth. Add enough remaining flour to form a firm dough.

2. Turn dough onto a floured surface; knead until smooth and elastic, about 6 minutes. Place in a greased bowl, turning once to grease top. Cover and let rise in a warm place until doubled, about 50 minutes.

3. Preheat oven to 400°. In a large skillet, cook sausage over medium heat until no longer pink; remove with a slotted spoon and set aside. Saute peppers and onion in drippings until tender; drain.

4. Press half of the dough onto the bottom and ½ in. up the sides of a greased 15x10x1-in. baking pan. Spread sausage evenly over crust. Top with peppers and onion. Sprinkle with mozzarella cheese. Roll out remaining dough to fit pan; place over cheese and seal edges.

5. In a bowl, beat the egg and water. Stir in the remaining ingredients. Brush over dough. Cut slits in top. Bake 20-25 minutes or until crust is golden brown. Cut into squares.

> As Sunday school teachers, my husband and I often host youth groups, so I dreamed up this handy recipe to feed some hungry teenagers. They loved this pizza-like sandwich and still request it when they visit.
>
> —**MARY MERRILL** BLOOMINGDALE, OH

HOT CRAB HERO

These sandwich slices add a hint of luxury to your brunch buffet or appetizer tray.
—**BEVERLY MIX** MISSOULA, MT

PREP: 15 MIN. • **BAKE:** 20 MIN.
MAKES: 12-14 SLICES

- 2 **cans (6 ounces each) crabmeat, drained, flaked and cartilage removed**
- ½ **cup mayonnaise**
- ¼ **cup minced fresh parsley**
- ¼ **cup sour cream**
- 1 **tablespoon lemon juice**
- ½ **teaspoon garlic powder**
- ⅛ **teaspoon salt**
- 1 **loaf (8 ounces) French bread**
- 2 **tablespoons butter, softened**
- 4 **slices Swiss cheese**

1. Preheat oven to 350°. In a large bowl, combine first seven ingredients. Slice bread horizontally in half; spread cut sides with butter. Top with cheese; spread with crab mixture.
2. Place on an ungreased baking sheet. Bake 20-25 minutes or until browned. Cut into slices.

OATMEAL BRULEE WITH GINGER CREAM

When it's chilly outside, warm up your family with my awesome oatmeal. I love the caramelized top and raspberry surprise.
—**YVONNE STARLIN** HERMITAGE, TN

PREP: 30 MIN. • **BROIL:** 10 MIN.
MAKES: 4 SERVINGS

GINGER CREAM
- ½ **cup heavy whipping cream**
- 2 **slices fresh gingerroot (about ¾-inch diameter)**
- 1 **cinnamon stick (3 inches)**
- 1 **tablespoon grated orange peel**
- 3 **tablespoons maple syrup**
- ⅛ **teaspoon ground nutmeg**

OATMEAL
- 4 **cups water**
- 2 **cups old-fashioned oats**
- ¼ **cup chopped dried apricots**
- ¼ **cup dried cherries, chopped**
- ½ **teaspoon salt**
- 3 **tablespoons brown sugar**
- 2 **tablespoons butter, softened**
- 1 **cup fresh or frozen unsweetened raspberries, thawed**
- ¼ **cup sugar**

1. In a saucepan, bring cream, ginger, cinnamon stick and orange peel to a boil. Reduce heat; simmer, covered, 10 minutes. Remove from heat; strain and discard solids. Stir in syrup and nutmeg.
2. In a large saucepan, bring water to a boil; stir in the oats, apricots, cherries and salt. Reduce heat to medium; cook 5 minutes, stirring occasionally. Remove from heat; stir in the brown sugar and ¼ cup ginger cream. Let stand, covered, 2 minutes.
3. Grease four 10-oz. broiler-safe ramekins with butter; place on a baking sheet. Divide raspberries among the ramekins. Spoon the oatmeal over raspberries; sprinkle evenly with sugar. Broil 4-6 in. from heat 7-9 minutes or until sugar is caramelized. Serve with remaining ginger cream.

STORING GINGER

Unpeeled gingerroot can be frozen in a resealable plastic freezer bag for up to 1 year. When needed, simply peel and grate or chop the amount required.

Oatmeal Brulee
with Ginger Cream

CALIFORNIA CASSEROLE

We may be from Texas but we sure enjoy eating this colorful casserole named after a West Coast state. It's compatible with a variety of side dishes.

—HOPE LASHIER AMARILLO, TX

PREP: 20 MIN. • **BAKE:** 1 HOUR
MAKES: 12-16 SERVINGS

- 8 **ounces wide egg noodles**
- 2 **pounds ground beef**
- 1 **medium green pepper, chopped**
- ¾ **cup chopped onion**
- 1 **can (14¾ ounces) cream-style corn**
- 1 **can (10¾ ounces) condensed tomato soup, undiluted**
- 1 **can (10 ounces) tomatoes with green chilies, undrained**
- 1 **can (8 ounces) tomato sauce**
- 1 **jar (4½ ounces) whole mushrooms, drained**
- 1 **jar (4 ounces) chopped pimientos, drained**
- 1 **can (2¼ ounces) sliced ripe olives, drained**
- 1½ **teaspoons celery salt**
- ½ **teaspoon ground mustard**
- ½ **teaspoon chili powder**
- ¼ **teaspoon pepper**
- 2 **cups (8 ounces) shredded cheddar cheese**

1. Cook the noodles according to package directions.

2. Meanwhile, preheat oven to 350°. In a large skillet, cook beef, green pepper and onion over medium heat until meat is no longer pink and vegetables are tender; drain. Stir in the corn, soup, tomatoes, tomato sauce, mushrooms, pimientos, olives and seasonings. Drain noodles and add to skillet.

3. Pour into a greased 13x9-in. baking dish. Cover and bake 50 minutes. Sprinkle with cheese; bake 10 minutes longer or until cheese is melted.

VEGGIE CALZONES

Bread dough makes it a breeze to assemble these savory turnovers. They freeze well, and once frozen, they can be heated in half an hour. If you have a favorite pizza dough, use it instead.

—LEE ANN AREY GRAY, ME

PREP: 25 MIN. + RISING • **BAKE:** 35 MIN.
MAKES: 8 SERVINGS

- ½ **pound fresh mushrooms, chopped**
- 1 **medium onion, chopped**
- 1 **medium green pepper, chopped**
- 2 **tablespoons canola oil**
- 3 **plum tomatoes, seeded and chopped**
- 1 **can (6 ounces) tomato paste**
- 1 **cup (4 ounces) shredded Monterey Jack cheese**
- 1 **cup (4 ounces) shredded part-skim mozzarella cheese**
- ½ **cup grated Parmesan cheese**
- 2 **loaves (1 pound each) frozen bread dough, thawed**
- 1 **egg**
- 1 **tablespoon water**

1. In a large skillet, saute mushrooms, onion and green pepper in oil until tender. Add tomatoes; cook and stir 3 minutes. Stir in tomato paste; set aside. Combine cheeses and set aside.
2. On a lightly floured surface, divide dough into eight pieces. Roll each piece into a 7-in. circle. Spoon a scant ½ cup of vegetable mixture and ¼ of cup of cheese mixture over one side of each circle. Brush edges of dough with water; fold dough over filling and press edges with a fork to seal. Place calzones 3 in. apart on greased baking sheets. Cover and let rise in a warm place 20 minutes.
3. Preheat oven to 375°. Whisk the egg and water; brush over calzones. Bake 33-37 minutes.

FREEZE OPTION *Bake calzones 15 minutes and cool. Place in a resealable freezer bag. Seal bag and freeze up to 3 months. To use, preheat oven to 350°. Place frozen calzones 2 in. apart on a greased baking sheet. Bake 30-35 minutes or until golden brown.*

BREAKFAST RICE PUDDING

My husband makes this rice pudding quite often for breakfast. It's equally good with fresh blueberries instead of cherries.

—SUE DRAHEIM WATERFORD, WI

PREP: 15 MIN. • **BAKE:** 25 MIN.
MAKES: 8 SERVINGS

- 1⅓ **cups uncooked long grain or basmati rice**
- 1 **can (15¼ ounces) peach halves, drained**
- 1 **cup canned or frozen pitted tart cherries, drained**
- 1 **cup heavy whipping cream**
- ½ **cup packed brown sugar, divided**
- ¼ **cup old-fashioned oats**
- ¼ **cup flaked coconut**
- ¼ **cup chopped pecans**
- ¼ **cup butter, melted**

1. Cook rice according to package directions.
2. Preheat oven to 375°. In a large bowl, combine rice, peaches, cherries, cream and ¼ cup brown sugar. Transfer to a greased 1½-qt. baking dish.
3. Combine oats, coconut, pecans, butter and remaining brown sugar; sprinkle over rice. Bake, uncovered, 25-30 minutes or until golden brown.

MAPLE-BACON GRITS PUFF

Bacon and maple add salty sweetness to a grits dish that puffs, tastes yummy and is beautiful to look at.
—**LOTTE WASHBURN** SEBRING, FL

PREP: 20 MIN. • **BAKE:** 1 HOUR
MAKES: 8 SERVINGS

- 8 **bacon strips, chopped**
- 2 **cups 2% milk**
- 1¼ **cups water**
- ½ **teaspoon salt**
- 1 **cup quick-cooking grits**
- ½ **cup maple syrup**
- 4 **eggs, lightly beaten**
  Minced fresh chives, optional

1. Preheat oven to 350°. In a large skillet, cook the bacon over medium heat until crisp, stirring occasionally. Remove with a slotted spoon; drain on paper towels. Reserve 2 tablespoons of the drippings.
2. In a large saucepan, bring milk, water and salt to a boil. Slowly stir in grits. Reduce heat to medium-low; cook, covered, 5-7 minutes or until thickened, stirring occasionally. Remove from heat; stir in maple syrup, half of the cooked bacon and reserved drippings.
3. In a bowl, whisk a small amount of hot grits into eggs until blended; return all to pan, mixing well. Transfer to a greased 8-in.-square baking dish.
4. Bake, uncovered, 1 hour or until a knife inserted near the center comes out clean. Sprinkle with remaining bacon and, if desired, chives; let stand 5 minutes before serving.

FAVORITE COMPANY CASSEROLE

Even my friends who don't eat a lot of broccoli or mushrooms admit that this casserole is a winner. It's so easy to throw together, and the leftovers are delicious.
—**SUZANN VERDUN** LISLE, IL

PREP: 15 MIN. • **BAKE:** 45 MIN.
MAKES: 8 SERVINGS

- 1 **package (6 ounces) wild rice, cooked**
- 3 **cups frozen chopped broccoli, thawed**
- 1½ **cups cubed cooked chicken**
- 1 **cup cubed cooked ham**
- 1 **cup (4 ounces) shredded cheddar cheese**
- 1 **jar (4½ ounces) sliced mushrooms, drained**
- 1 **cup mayonnaise**
- 1 **teaspoon prepared mustard**
- ½ **to 1 teaspoon curry powder**
- 1 **can (10¾ ounces) condensed cream of mushroom soup, undiluted**
- ¼ **cup grated Parmesan cheese**

1. Preheat oven to 350°. In a greased 2-qt. baking dish, layer the first six ingredients in order listed. Combine mayonnaise, mustard, curry and soup. Spread over top. Sprinkle with the Parmesan cheese.
2. Bake, uncovered, 45-60 minutes or until top is light golden brown.

HAM ON BISCUITS

I enjoy entertaining friends at a brunch or lunch. They always compliment me on these special little ham sandwiches made on cheesy homemade biscuits. Usually I use Smithfield ham, but if salty ham is not your preference, any thin-sliced ham works well.

—**BETSY HEDEMAN** TIMONIUM, MD

START TO FINISH: 30 MIN.
MAKES: 8 SANDWICHES

- 1   cup all-purpose flour
- 2   teaspoons sugar
- 1⅛ teaspoons baking powder
- ¼   teaspoon baking soda
- ⅛   teaspoon salt
- 2   tablespoons cold butter
- ½   cup 4% cottage cheese
- 1   egg
- 3   tablespoons milk
- 8   teaspoons butter, softened
- ½   pound sliced deli ham

1. Preheat oven to 450°. In a small bowl, combine flour, sugar, baking powder, baking soda and salt; cut in cold butter until mixture resembles coarse crumbs. In a small bowl, beat cottage cheese 2 minutes. Beat in egg and milk until blended. Stir into crumb mixture just until moistened.

2. Turn dough onto a lightly floured surface; knead 8-10 times. Pat or roll dough out to ½-in. thickness; cut out eight biscuits with a floured 2½-in. biscuit cutter.

3. Place 1 in. apart on an ungreased baking sheet. Bake 8-12 minutes or until golden brown. Split biscuits in half; spread with softened butter. Place ham on biscuit bottoms; replace tops.

CREAMY CHICKEN NOODLE BAKE

Talk about a potluck pleaser! This creamy, comforting casserole is bursting with tender chunks of chicken.

—**SHIRLEY UNGER** BLUFFTON, OH

PREP: 25 MIN. • **BAKE:** 40 MIN. + STANDING
MAKES: 12 SERVINGS (1 CUP EACH)

- 4   cups uncooked egg noodles
- ½   cup butter, divided
- ¼   cup all-purpose flour
- ½   teaspoon salt
- ⅛   teaspoon white pepper
- 3½ cups 2% milk
- 4   cups cubed cooked chicken
- 2   jars (12 ounces each) chicken gravy
- 1   jar (2 ounces) diced pimientos, drained
- ½   cup cubed process cheese (Velveeta)
- ½   cup dry bread crumbs
- 4   teaspoons butter, melted

1. Cook the noodles according to package directions.

2. Meanwhile, preheat oven to 350°. In a Dutch oven, melt 6 tablespoons butter. Stir in flour, salt and pepper until smooth. Gradually add milk. Bring to a boil; cook and stir 1-2 minutes or until thickened. Remove from heat. Stir in chicken, gravy and pimientos.

3. Drain noodles; toss with remaining butter. Stir into chicken mixture. Pour into a greased 13x9-in. baking dish.

4. Cover and bake 30-35 minutes or until bubbly. Combine cheese, bread crumbs and melted butter. Sprinkle around edges of casserole. Bake, uncovered, 10 minutes longer or until golden brown. Let stand 10 minutes before serving.

ARTICHOKE SHRIMP BAKE

You can substitute frozen asparagus cuts for the artichoke hearts and cream of asparagus soup for cream of shrimp in my special-occasion casserole. I usually serve it with rice, but it's also nice with fresh homemade biscuits.

—JEANNE HOLT MENDOTA HEIGHTS, MN

PREP: 20 MIN. • **BAKE:** 20 MIN.
MAKES: 4 SERVINGS

- 1 **pound cooked medium shrimp, peeled and deveined**
- 1 **can (14 ounces) water-packed artichoke hearts, rinsed, drained and quartered**
- ⅔ **cup frozen pearl onions, thawed**
- 2 **cups sliced fresh mushrooms**
- 1 **small sweet red pepper, chopped**
- 2 **tablespoons butter**
- 1 **can (10¾ ounces) condensed cream of shrimp soup, undiluted**
- ½ **cup sour cream**
- ¼ **cup sherry or chicken broth**
- 2 **teaspoons Worcestershire sauce**
- 1 **teaspoon grated lemon peel**
- ⅛ **teaspoon white pepper**

TOPPING

- ½ **cup soft bread crumbs**
- ⅓ **cup grated Parmesan cheese**
- 1 **tablespoon minced fresh parsley**
- 1 **tablespoon butter, melted**
  Hot cooked rice, optional

1. Preheat oven to 375°. Place shrimp, artichokes and onions in a greased 11x7-in. baking dish; set aside.

2. In a large skillet, saute mushrooms and red pepper in butter until tender. Stir in the soup, sour cream, sherry, Worcestershire sauce, lemon peel and white pepper; heat through. Pour over shrimp mixture.

3. In a small bowl, combine bread crumbs, cheese, parsley and butter; sprinkle over top.

4. Bake, uncovered, 20-25 minutes or until bubbly and topping is golden brown. Serve with rice if desired.

BRUNCH NOTES

FOUR-CHEESE BAKED PENNE

Rich and cheesy with a slight heat from pepper flakes, this meatless pasta dish is packed with protein.

—SCARLETT ELROD NEWNAN, GA

PREP: 30 MIN. + COOLING • **BAKE:** 20 MIN.
MAKES: 6 SERVINGS

- 4 **cups uncooked whole wheat penne pasta**
- 1 **medium onion, chopped**
- 2 **teaspoons olive oil**
- 4 **garlic cloves, minced**
- 1 **can (15 ounces) crushed tomatoes**
- 1 **can (8 ounces) tomato sauce**
- 3 **tablespoons minced fresh parsley or 1 tablespoon dried parsley flakes**
- 1 **teaspoon dried oregano**
- 1 **teaspoon dried rosemary, crushed**
- ½ **teaspoon crushed red pepper flakes**
- ¼ **teaspoon pepper**
- 1½ **cups (12 ounces) 2% cottage cheese**
- 1¼ **cups (5 ounces) shredded part-skim mozzarella cheese, divided**
- 1 **cup part-skim ricotta cheese**
- ¼ **cup grated Parmesan cheese**

1. Cook penne according to the package directions.

2. Meanwhile, in a large skillet, saute onion in oil until tender. Add garlic; cook 1 minute longer. Stir in the tomatoes, tomato sauce, parsley, oregano, rosemary, pepper flakes and pepper. Bring to a boil. Remove from heat; cool 15 minutes.

3. Preheat oven to 400°. Drain penne; add to sauce. Stir in the cottage cheese, 1/2 cup mozzarella and all of the ricotta. Transfer to a 13x9-in. baking dish coated with cooking spray. Top with the Parmesan cheese and the remaining mozzarella.

4. Bake, uncovered, 20-25 minutes or until the casserole is bubbly.

Caramel-Pecan
Apple Slices

Sunshine Bright
Fruits & Sides

CARAMEL-PECAN APPLE SLICES

START TO FINISH: 15 MIN.
MAKES: 6 SERVINGS

- ⅓ **cup packed brown sugar**
- 2 **tablespoons butter**
- 2 **large apples, cut into ½-inch slices**
- ¼ **cup chopped pecans, toasted**

In a large skillet, cook and stir brown sugar and butter over medium heat until sugar is dissolved. Add apples; cook, uncovered, over medium heat 5-7 minutes or until tender, stirring occasionally. Stir in pecans. Serve warm.

NOTE *To toast nuts, spread them in a 15x10x1-in. baking pan. Bake at 350° for 5-10 minutes or until lightly browned, stirring occasionally. Or, spread in a dry nonstick skillet and heat over low heat until lightly browned, stirring occasionally.*

Here's a warm, decadent side dish for a winter brunch. Ready to eat in only 15 minutes, the apples are also good alongside a pork entree or spooned over vanilla ice cream.

—**CAROL GILLESPIE** CHAMBERSBURG, PA

FRUIT CUP WITH CITRUS SAUCE

This medley of fresh fruits is so elegant that I serve it in my prettiest crystal bowls. With its dressed-up flavor, it's perfect for a special event.

—**EDNA LEE** GREELEY, CO

PREP: 10 MIN. + CHILLING
MAKES: 6 SERVINGS

- ¾ **cup orange juice**
- ¼ **cup white wine or white grape juice**
- 2 **tablespoons lemon juice**
- 1 **tablespoon sugar**
- 1½ **cups cantaloupe balls**
- 1 **cup halved green grapes**
- 1 **cup halved fresh strawberries**
  Fresh mint, optional

1. In a small bowl, combine orange juice, wine or grape juice, lemon juice and sugar; mix well. In a large bowl, combine the fruit; add juice mixture and toss to coat.

2. Cover and refrigerate 2-3 hours, stirring occasionally. If desired, garnish with mint.

COCONUT TROPICAL FRUIT SALAD

Add a serving of fruit to a breakfast with this delicious medley. Toasted coconut, mango and more bring the flavor of the tropics indoors.

—**KATIE COVINGTON** BLACKSBURG, SC

START TO FINISH: 25 MIN.
MAKES: 8 SERVINGS

- 1 **medium mango, peeled and cubed**
- 1 **medium green apple, cubed**
- 1 **medium red apple, cubed**
- 1 **medium pear, cubed**
- 1 **medium navel orange, peeled and chopped**
- 2 **medium kiwifruit, peeled and chopped**
- 10 **seedless red grapes, halved**
- 2 **tablespoons orange juice**
- 1 **firm medium banana, sliced**
- ¼ **cup flaked coconut, toasted**

In a large bowl, combine the first seven ingredients. Drizzle with orange juice; toss gently to coat. Refrigerate until serving. Just before serving, fold in banana and sprinkle with coconut.
NOTE *To toast coconut, spread in a dry nonstick skillet and heat over low heat until lightly browned, stirring occasionally.*

PEACHES 'N' CREAM CUPS

For a no-fuss treat that's as cool and refreshing as a summer breeze, try these tasty cups with a gingersnap crust and creamy yogurt filling.

—**SUZANNE MCKINLEY** LYONS, GA

PREP: 10 MIN. + CHILLING
MAKES: 2 SERVINGS

- 1 **gingersnap cookie, crumbled**
- ¼ **teaspoon ground ginger**
- ¾ **cup (6 ounces) peach yogurt**
- ¼ **cup cream cheese, softened**
- ¼ **teaspoon vanilla extract**
- ⅓ **cup sliced peaches, drained and chopped**

1. In a small bowl, combine crumbs and ginger; set aside. In a small bowl, beat the yogurt, cream cheese and vanilla until smooth. Fold in peaches.
2. Spoon into two 6-oz. custard cups; cover and refrigerate 1 hour. Just before serving, sprinkle with the reserved crumb mixture.

TASTE OF HAWAII YOGURT

Plain yogurt becomes a flavorful sensation with help from coconut extract, pineapple and a hint of lime.

—*TASTE OF HOME* **TEST KITCHEN**

START TO FINISH: 5 MIN.
MAKES: 4 SERVINGS

- 2 **cups (16 ounces) reduced-fat plain yogurt**
- 1 **can (8 ounces) unsweetened crushed pineapple, drained**
- 2 **teaspoons sugar**
- ¼ **teaspoon coconut extract**
- ¼ **teaspoon grated lime peel**

In a small bowl, combine all ingredients. Chill until serving.

MUSHROOM HASH BROWNS

When you have leftover veggies, toss them into the skillet to brighten this dish up! We like to serve the finished product with a garnish of sour cream.

—JENNIFER BISTLINE CONFLUENCE, PA

PREP: 20 MIN. • **COOK:** 15 MIN.
MAKES: 4 SERVINGS

- 1 **small onion, finely chopped**
- ½ **cup sliced fresh mushrooms**
- ½ **cup chopped green pepper**
- 1 **tablespoon canola oil**
- 3 **cups frozen shredded hash brown potatoes**
- 1 **medium tomato, finely chopped**
- ½ **cup shredded reduced-fat cheddar cheese**
- 2 **tablespoons sliced ripe olives**
- 1 **jalapeno pepper, seeded and sliced**
- ¼ **teaspoon seasoned salt**
- ⅛ **teaspoon pepper**
- 1 **tablespoon minced chives**

1. In a large nonstick skillet, saute the onion, mushrooms and green pepper in oil until tender. Add hash browns; cook over medium heat for 8-10 minutes or until potatoes are browned, stirring occasionally.

2. Stir in the tomato, cheese, olives, jalapeno, seasoned salt and pepper. Cover and cook 2 minutes or until cheese is melted. Sprinkle with chives; cut into wedges.

NOTE *Wear disposable gloves when cutting hot peppers; the oils can burn skin. Avoid touching your face.*

MORNING FRUIT SALAD

My best friend made this refreshing salad for lunch one hot summer day. It was so good, I just had to have the recipe. Now I make it every chance I get. It's always a hit at picnics and church brunches.

—**NIKKI GAINES** COVINGTON, GA

START TO FINISH: 25 MIN.
MAKES: 6-8 SERVINGS

- 1 **can (11 ounces) mandarin oranges**
- ¼ **cup plus 2 tablespoons mayonnaise**
- 1½ **cups seedless grapes, halved**
- 2 **small apples, chopped**
- 2 **small bananas, sliced**
- ⅓ **cup flaked coconut**
- ⅓ **cup chopped walnuts**
- ¼ **cup maraschino cherries, halved**
- ¼ **cup raisins**

1. Drain the oranges, reserving 4½ teaspoons juice (discard remaining juice or save for another use). In a small bowl, combine the mayonnaise and reserved juice.

2. In a large bowl, mix oranges, grapes, apples, bananas, coconut, walnuts, cherries and raisins. Divide among serving dishes; drizzle with mayonnaise mixture. Serve immediately.

EASY POTATO PANCAKES

Using frozen hash browns makes Easy Potato Pancakes a snap to fix. They are a tasty companion to eggs.

—**MARLENE HARGUTH** MAYNARD, MN

START TO FINISH: 20 MIN.
MAKES: 4 SERVINGS

- 3 **cups frozen shredded hash brown potatoes**
- 2 **tablespoons all-purpose flour**
- 2 **eggs, lightly beaten**
- 3 **tablespoons butter, melted**
- 1½ **teaspoons water**
- ½ **teaspoon salt**
- 1 **tablespoon canola oil**

1. Place the hash browns in a strainer; rinse with cold water until thawed. Drain thoroughly; transfer to a large bowl. Add the flour, eggs, butter, water and salt and mix well.

2. Heat the oil in a large skillet over medium heat. Drop batter by ⅓ cupfuls into oil; fry until golden brown on both sides. Drain on paper towels.

BRUNCH NOTES

HINT OF MINT FRUIT SALAD

I love making herbal syrups like the simple dressing for this colorful fruit salad. It definitely adds pizzazz to our meal.

—SUE GRONHOLZ BEAVER DAM, WI

PREP: 20 MIN. + CHILLING
MAKES: 12 SERVINGS

- 1 **cup sugar**
- 1 **cup water**
- 1 **cup loosely packed mint sprigs**
- 2½ **cups chopped apples**
- 2½ **cups chopped ripe pears**
- 2 **cups cubed fresh pineapple**
- 2 **cups sliced fresh strawberries**
- 1 **cup fresh blueberries**
- 1 **cup mayonnaise**

1. In a large saucepan, bring sugar and water to a boil. Reduce heat; simmer, uncovered, 4 minutes. Remove from heat. Add the mint; cover and steep 20 minutes. Strain, discarding mint. Transfer the syrup to a small bowl; refrigerate until chilled.

2. Just before serving, combine the apples, pears, pineapple, strawberries and blueberries in a large bowl. Stir mayonnaise into mint syrup until blended; pour over fruit and toss to coat.

SELECTING FRESH FRUITS

No matter what fruit you are buying, look it over before placing it in your cart. Fruit bruises easily, so handle it with care. Avoid buying any that are bruised, withered, off-colored or crushed; they will spoil quickly.

Hint of Mint Fruit Salad

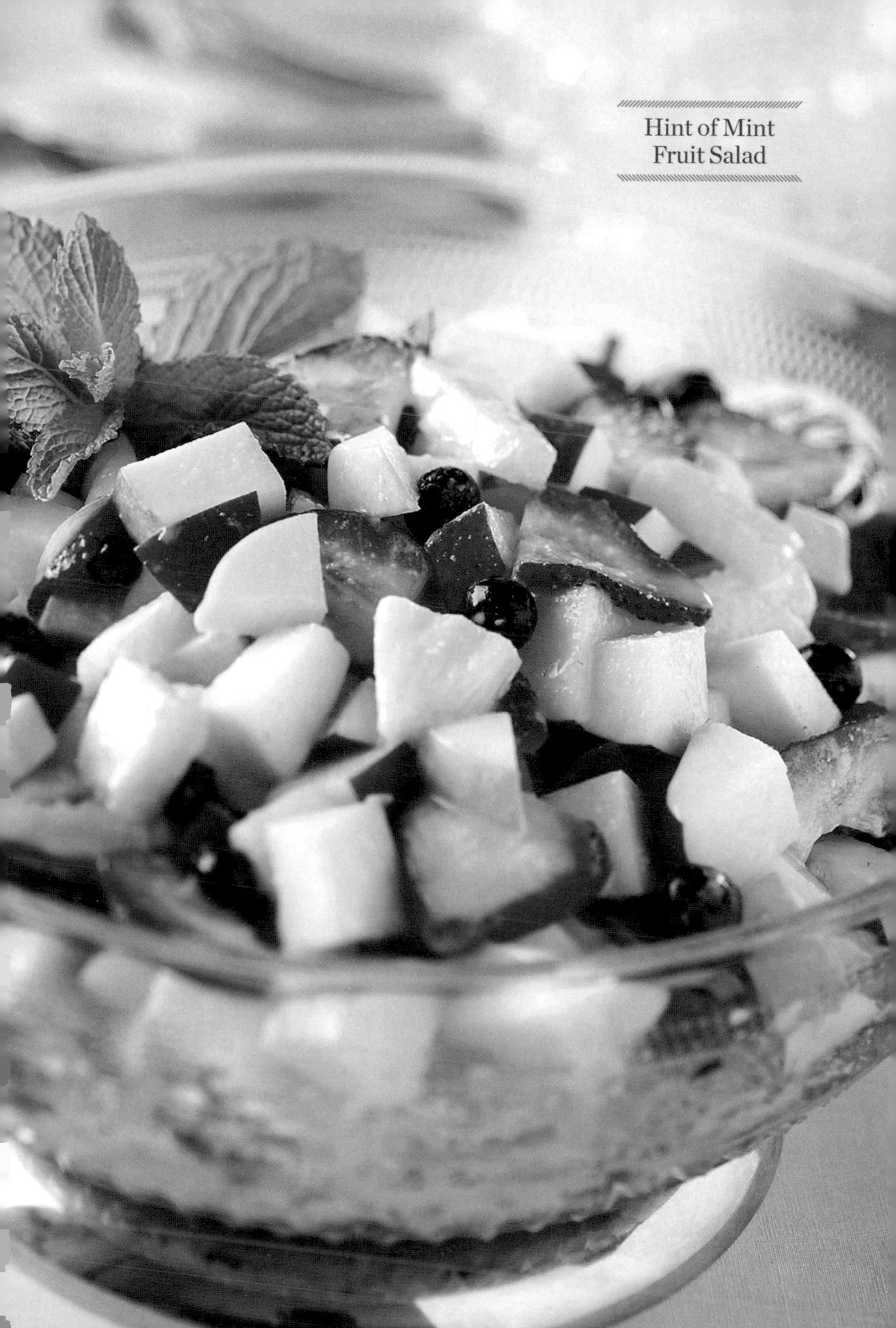

HOT FRUIT COMPOTE

This sweet and colorful fruit compote is perfect with an egg casserole at a brunch. It can bake right alongside the eggs, so everything is conveniently done at the same time.

—JOYCE MOYNIHAN LAKEVILLE, MN

PREP: 15 MIN. • **BAKE:** 40 MIN.
MAKES: 20 SERVINGS

- 2 **cans (15¼ ounces each) sliced pears, drained**
- 1 **can (29 ounces) sliced peaches, drained**
- 1 **can (20 ounces) unsweetened pineapple chunks, drained**
- 1 **package (20 ounces) pitted dried plums**
- 1 **jar (16 ounces) unsweetened applesauce**
- 1 **can (21 ounces) cherry pie filling**
- ¼ **cup packed brown sugar**

1. Preheat oven to 350°. In a large bowl, mix the first five ingredients. Pour into a 13x9-in. baking dish coated with cooking spray. Spread the pie filling over fruit mixture; sprinkle with the brown sugar.
2. Cover and bake 40-45 minutes or until bubbly. Serve warm.

FRUIT SLUSH

As a busy mom, I try to do all that I can before company arrives. This sweet citrus slush is easy to make ahead and tastes so refreshing. I often add red seedless grapes.

—MARTHA MILLER FREDERICKSBURG, OH

PREP: 20 MIN. + FREEZING
MAKES: 6-8 SERVINGS

- 3 **cups water**
- 1 **cup sugar**
- 1 **can (20 ounces) crushed pineapple, undrained**
- 1 **can (6 ounces) frozen orange juice concentrate, thawed**
- 1 **medium ripe peach, chopped or ⅔ cup sliced frozen peaches, thawed and chopped**

1. In a large saucepan over medium heat, bring water and sugar to a boil. Remove from heat. Cool 10 minutes.
2. Add the pineapple, orange juice concentrate and peach; stir well. Pour into a freezer container and freeze at least 12 hours or overnight (may be frozen up to 3 months). Remove from the freezer 1 hour before serving.

SWEET BERRY BRUSCHETTA

Sometimes I've made this recipe by toasting the bread on a grill at cookouts, but any way I serve it, I never have any leftovers. The bruschetta is sweet instead of savory, and guests enjoy the change.

—PATRICIA NIEH PORTOLA VALLEY, CA

START TO FINISH: 20 MIN.
MAKES: 10 PIECES

- 10 **slices French bread (½ inch thick)**
  Cooking spray
- 5 **teaspoons sugar, divided**
- 6 **ounces fat-free cream cheese**
- ½ **teaspoon almond extract**
- ¾ **cup fresh blackberries**
- ¾ **cup fresh raspberries**
- ¼ **cup slivered almonds, toasted**
- 2 **teaspoons confectioners' sugar**

1. Place bread on an ungreased baking sheet; lightly coat with cooking spray. Sprinkle with 2 teaspoons sugar. Broil 3-4 in. from heat 1-2 minutes or until lightly browned.

2. In a small bowl, mix cream cheese, extract and remaining sugar. Spread over toasted bread. Top with berries and almonds; dust with confectioners' sugar. Serve immediately.

Hawaiian
Fruit Salad

HAWAIIAN FRUIT SALAD

This salad says summer to me because it's so light and colorful. The banana dressing tops it off with a flair, and you can use a little extra sour cream for a pretty presentation.

—PAT HABIGER SPEARVILLE, KS

START TO FINISH: 30 MIN.
MAKES: 14 SERVINGS

- 3½ cups cubed fresh pineapple
- 3 cups honeydew balls
- 1½ cups cantaloupe balls
- 1 medium mango, peeled and cubed
- 1 cup green grapes
- 1 cup halved fresh strawberries
- 1 kiwifruit, peeled, quartered and sliced

BANANA DRESSING

- 2 small bananas, cut into 1-inch pieces
- 1 cup (8 ounces) reduced-fat sour cream
- ¼ cup packed brown sugar
- 1½ teaspoons lemon juice

In a large bowl, combine the first seven ingredients. In a food processor, combine the bananas, sour cream, brown sugar and lemon juice. Cover and process until smooth. Serve the dressing with the fruit.

OTHER USES FOR A MELON BALLER

Do you hate to buy a utensil or gadget for only one use? Well, a melon baller can be used to make balls of butter or small scoops of ice cream for garnishes. It can also be used to remove seeds and pulp from cherry tomatoes, cucumbers or squash.

BROILED GRAPEFRUIT

This easy-to-prepare dish lends eye-catching appeal to a winter breakfast or brunch. Brown sugar sweetens the tart fruit. If you have the time, definitely make the sugared grapes. They add a classy accent to the grapefruit.

—**VICKI HOLLOWAY** JOELTON, TN

START TO FINISH: 25 MIN.
MAKES: 10 SERVINGS

- 5 **medium pink grapefruit**
- ¼ **cup packed brown sugar**
- 2 **tablespoons plus ¼ cup sugar, divided**
- 2 **tablespoons butter, melted**
   Seedless red and green grape clusters

1. Cut each grapefruit in half horizontally. With a sharp knife, cut around each section to loosen fruit. Place grapefruit halves, cut side up, in a 15x10x1-in. baking pan.

2. Mix brown sugar and 2 tablespoons sugar; sprinkle over grapefruit. Drizzle with butter. Broil 4 in. from heat until sugar is bubbly.

3. For garnish, rinse grape clusters and dip in remaining sugar. Place on grapefruit; serve warm.

ABOUT GRAPEFRUIT

Grapefruit are available in white (yellow-white pulp) or pink, which can range in color from pale pink to red. The pink varieties are higher in Vitamin A than the white varieties. Grapefruit can be refrigerated in a plastic bag up to 2 weeks.

POLYNESIAN PARFAITS

Pack one of these fruity treats in a plastic container to take with you on a hectic morning. The yummy parfaits are ideal for lunch boxes, too.

—**JANICE MITCHELL** AURORA, CO

START TO FINISH: 15 MIN.
MAKES: 4 SERVINGS

- 2 **cups (16 ounces) pineapple yogurt**
- 1 **tablespoon sugar**
- ⅛ **teaspoon ground nutmeg**
- 1 **cup granola without raisins**
- 1 **can (11 ounces) mandarin oranges, drained**
- ¾ **cup unsweetened pineapple tidbits**
- ⅓ **cup fresh raspberries**

Combine the yogurt, sugar and nutmeg; spoon into four dishes. Top with granola and fruit.

VANILLA FRUIT SALAD

Peach pie filling is the secret ingredient in this crowd-pleasing salad. Make it throughout the year using whatever fruits are in season.

—**NANCY DODSON** SPRINGFIELD, IL

START TO FINISH: 20 MIN.
MAKES: 10 SERVINGS

- 1 **pound fresh strawberries, quartered**
- 1½ **cups seedless red and/or green grapes, halved**
- 2 **medium bananas, sliced**
- 2 **kiwifruit, peeled, sliced and quartered**
- 1 **cup cubed fresh pineapple**
- 1 **can (21 ounces) peach pie filling**
- 3 **teaspoons vanilla extract**

In a large bowl, mix the first five ingredients. Fold in pie filling and vanilla. Chill until serving.

BERRY & YOGURT PHYLLO NESTS

This elegant presentation lends a special touch to any meal. Add variety by using your favorite combination of flavored yogurt and berries.
—*TASTE OF HOME* **TEST KITCHEN**

PREP: 25 MIN. + COOLING
MAKES: 6 SERVINGS

- 6 **sheets phyllo dough (14x9 inches)**
   Butter-flavored cooking spray
- 2½ **teaspoons sugar, divided**
- ⅓ **cup vanilla yogurt**
- 1 **teaspoon grated orange peel**
- 1 **teaspoon orange juice**
- ½ **cup halved fresh strawberries**
- ½ **cup fresh raspberries**
- ½ **cup fresh blueberries**
   Fresh mint leaves, optional

1. Place one sheet of phyllo dough on a work surface; spritz with the butter-flavored spray. Top with another sheet of phyllo; spritz with spray. Cut into six squares. (Keep the remaining phyllo covered with plastic wrap and a damp towel to prevent it from drying out.) Repeat with the remaining phyllo.
2. Stack three squares of layered phyllo in each of six muffin cups coated with cooking spray, rotating squares so corners do not overlap. Sprinkle ¼ teaspoon sugar into each cup. Spritz with cooking spray. Bake at 375° for 6-8 minutes or until golden brown. Cool on a wire rack.
3. Meanwhile, in a small bowl, whisk yogurt, orange peel, orange juice and the remaining sugar. Spoon yogurt mixture into cups; top with berries. Garnish with mint if desired.

BANANA FRUIT COMPOTE

My mother used to make this recipe when I was a child. My four kids always ate more fruit when I dressed it up this way.
—**MAXINE OTIS** HOBSON, MT

PREP: 20 MIN. + CHILLING
MAKES: 2 SERVINGS

- 1 **cup apricot nectar, divided**
   Dash to ⅛ teaspoon ground cloves
   Dash to ⅛ teaspoon ground cinnamon
- 1 **tablespoon cornstarch**
- 2 **tablespoons lemon juice**
- 1 **firm banana, cut into ½-inch slices**
- 4 **fresh strawberries, sliced**
- 1 **kiwifruit, halved and thinly sliced**

1. In a small saucepan, bring ¾ cup apricot nectar, cloves and cinnamon to a boil. Combine cornstarch and the remaining apricot nectar until smooth; gradually whisk into nectar mixture. Return to a boil; cook and stir for 1-2 minutes or until thickened and bubbly. Remove from heat; stir in the lemon juice. Cool.
2. Stir in banana, strawberries and kiwi. Cover and refrigerate at least 1 hour before serving.

BRUNCH NOTES

_____
_____
_____
_____
_____
_____
_____
_____
_____
_____
_____
_____
_____
_____
_____
_____
_____
_____
_____
_____
_____
_____
_____
_____
_____
_____
_____
_____
_____
_____
_____
_____
_____
_____
_____
_____

LEMON BREAKFAST PARFAITS

PREP: 25 MIN. + COOLING • **MAKES:** 6 SERVINGS

- ¾ cup fat-free milk
  Dash salt
- ⅓ cup uncooked couscous
- ½ cup reduced-fat sour cream
- ½ cup lemon yogurt
- 1 tablespoon honey
- ¼ teaspoon grated lemon peel
- 1 cup fresh blueberries
- 1 cup fresh raspberries
- 1 cup sliced peeled kiwifruit
  Chopped crystallized ginger and minced
  fresh mint

1. In a small saucepan, bring milk and salt to a boil. Stir in couscous. Remove from heat; cover and let stand 5-10 minutes or until milk is absorbed. Fluff with a fork; cool.

2. In a small bowl, combine sour cream, yogurt, honey and lemon peel. Stir in couscous.

3. Combine blueberries and raspberries; spoon ¼ cup into each of six parfait glasses. Top with half the kiwi. Layer with couscous mixture and remaining berries and kiwi. Garnish with ginger and mint.

I serve these lively, layered parfaits as a refreshing start to a day. You can make the couscous mixture ahead, cover and chill overnight.
—JANELLE LEE APPLETON, WI

Lemon Breakfast
Parfaits

General Index

· Alphabetical Index ·